E. M. FORSTER:

THE PERILS OF HUMANISM

"It is difficult for most of us to
realise both the importance and the
unimportance of reason. But it is a
difficulty which the profounder
humanists have managed to solve."

— FORSTER, *Goldsworthy Lowes Dickinson.*

"And if thou gaze too long into an abyss,
the abyss will also gaze into thee."

— NIETZSCHE, *Beyond Good and Evil.*

E. M. FORSTER:

The Perils of Humanism

BY FREDERICK C. CREWS

PRINCETON, NEW JERSEY
PRINCETON UNIVERSITY PRESS
1962

Publication of this book has been aided by
the Ford Foundation program to support publication,
through university presses,
of work in the humanities and social sciences.

Chapter 9, "The Limitations of Mythology,"
appeared originally as an article in *Comparative
Literature*, Spring 1960, copyright © 1960, by
Comparative Literature; Chapter 5, "*The Longest
Journey*," appeared originally as an article in
ELH, Dec. 1959, copyright © 1959, by *ELH*.

The quotations from the following works of
E. M. Forster are reprinted by permission of
Harcourt, Brace & World, Inc.: *A Passage to
India*, copyright © 1924 by Harcourt, Brace &
World, Inc., copyright © 1952 by E. M. Forster;
Aspects of the Novel, copyright © 1927 by
Harcourt, Brace & World, Inc., copyright ©
1955 by E. M. Forster; *Goldsworthy Lowes
Dickinson*, copyright © 1934 by E. M. Forster;
Abinger Harvest, copyright © 1936 by E. M.
Forster; *Two Cheers for Democracy*, copyright ©
1938, 1939, 1947, 1949, 1951 by E. M. Forster;
The Hill of Devi, copyright © 1953 by E. M.
Forster; *Marianne Thornton*, copyright © 1956
by E. M. Forster.

Printed in the United States of America
by Princeton University Press, Princeton, New Jersey

for Betty

Preface

The author wants to confess at the outset that this volume grows out of a doctoral dissertation. Such an admission usually braces the reader for a pedantically "objective" work in which trivial facts are substituted for judgments of value. It will, indeed, be obvious that I am guilty of treating E. M. Forster more soberly than he treats himself; he could only be distressed or amused at the ponderous historical machinery I have wheeled up to his door. Still, I hope it will be seen that my book is founded on a sympathy with Forster's art and a commitment to some of his basic attitudes.

I am much indebted to my thesis director, E. D. H. Johnson of Princeton, who put at my disposal his impressive background in British intellectual history. Several other scholars deserve thanks for valuable criticism of my work at various stages since 1957: Noël Annan, Richard Ludwig, John H. Raleigh, Mark Schorer, and Ian Watt. Mrs. Henry Lynn, Jr. has been my dependable typist. I am also grateful for a grant from the Samuel S. Fels Foundation Fund in 1957-1958, for a President's Faculty Fellowship from the University of California in the summer of 1960, and for a publication grant from the Ford Foundation.

FREDERICK C. CREWS

BERKELEY, CALIFORNIA
SPRING 1961

Contents

E. M. FORSTER:

THE PERILS OF HUMANISM

One

INTRODUCTORY

The novels of E. M. Forster have, for many years now, enjoyed a modestly growing reputation for excellence. Lionel Trilling's slim but incisive *E. M. Forster*, published in 1943, began a wave of renewed interest in a writer who had gradually slipped from prominence after the success of *A Passage to India* in 1924.[1] The wave has gathered force until *Howards End* and *A Passage to India*, Forster's most ambitious novels, have become widely accepted as "modern classics." Though Forster is still alive, this premature canonization is not at all to be wondered at; as a novelist he has given us nothing since *A Passage to India*, and there are many reasons for regarding that novel as his definitive fictional statement. Forster's literary activity since 1924 can strike us only as a series of footnotes, however brilliant, to a career whose real center lies in the first decade of the twentieth century—an era before the names of Proust and Joyce and Mann were widely known.

Forster is thus an Edwardian in point of time, and he is equally so in spirit. His outlook on the world and his literary manner were already thoroughly developed in that epoch and have passed through the subsequent years of turbulence and cataclysm with remarkably little modification. He is, as he once wrote, "what my age and my upbringing have made me,"[2] namely, a kind of lapsed Victorian of the upper middle class, whose intellectual loyalties have remained with the Cambridge he first knew in 1897. The various modern revolutions in physics,

[1] For the immediate effect of Trilling's book, see Morton Dauwen Zabel, "A Forster Revival," *The Nation*, CLVII (1943), 158f., and E. K. Brown, "The Revival of E. M. Forster," *Yale Review*, XXXIII (1944), 668-681.

[2] *Abinger Harvest* (New York, 1936), p. 65.

in psychology, in politics, even in literary style, have not escaped his intelligent notice, but they can scarcely be said to have influenced him deeply. His response to the explosion of the Victorian dream of benevolent progress has been a modest and orderly retreat to safer ground—to a tolerant individualism now unmixed with Utopian dreams, but nevertheless closer to Victorian ideals than to any of the popular creeds of today. Rather than conform to bad times, Forster prefers to remind us cheerfully that his views are atavistic.

The strength of Forster's resistance to the twentieth century is especially apparent when we place him beside some of his fellow writers. If Joyce, Lawrence, Pound, and the early Eliot represent the main current of the modern literary movement in English, we must admit that Forster's private stream runs in an older channel. These others were radical iconoclasts whose rejection of bourgeois-democratic life was violent and shattering. Equally shattering was their fragmentation of the polite cadences of Victorian literature. In seeing the falseness of the old psychology, they conceived a scorn for the *hypocrite lecteur*; their role as apocalyptic prophets, as nay-sayers to the boredom and specious rationality of modern life, demanded that they be obscure and idiosyncratic. Forster, in contrast, unashamedly calls himself a bourgeois and remains faithful to the tradition of calm intelligibility. He is anti-apocalyptic in both his politics and his literary sense. To some degree his novels return us to the congenial Victorian relationship between writer and reader, with its unspoken agreement over the usefulness of the sociable virtues and its apotheosis of the happy family. Though Forster's heroes struggle against "society" as a body of inhibitions, their revolt is never truly radical. Instead of exercising Stephen Dedalus' silence, exile, and cunning against the intruding world, they merely try to fit their individuality into the domestic scheme that awaits them. And Forster's ironical style, though it is unsparing in its probing at shams and half-truths, presupposes a confidence in the reader's sympathy and good judgment—a confidence that seemed quite archaic to the other writers I have named.

Forster's resistance to modernity may account for the fact that his novels, though they are almost universally esteemed, have never won him a cult of fanatical disciples. Unlike Joyce and Lawrence, he is rarely consulted for oracular sayings or glossed like scripture. With a few exceptions, critics have tended to explicate and admire his works without becoming heated over the possible merit of his ideas. Yet Forster decidedly *is* a novelist of ideas,[3] and didactic moral content is hardly less conspicuous in his work than in Lawrence's. Forster's persistent "moral" is that the life of affectionate personal relations, disengaged from political and religious zeal by means of a tolerant eclecticism, is supremely valuable. This is not a stirring creed; in fact, it is a warning against allowing oneself to be stirred by any creed. And the mildness of Forster's position is only reinforced by his manner of writing, which, as Stephen Spender has noted, curiously marries self-effacement and whimsicality with assertiveness and great precision.[4] Prophets and transvaluers of values take themselves more seriously than Forster does.

It is understandable, yet regrettable, that Forster's offhand manner has successfully disguised the historical weight that lies behind his governing ideas. To uphold a pure individualism, as Forster does, would seem to imply a rejection of every established tradition. Actually, Forster's attitudes were conceived

[3] Here I am in apparent disagreement with James McConkey, who denies the presence of ideas in Forster's novels. McConkey prefers to speak of literary techniques in their relation to the "tonal quality" of the "Forsterian voice." I gather, however, that the denial of ideas here is merely a precaution against narrowly "intentional" criticism, for McConkey later makes reference to "the stabilized Forsterian philosophic position." The differences between Forster the man and Forster the novelistic "voice" are not specified by McConkey, and I have been unable to decide what they might be. Forster's novels are often so explicitly moral and philosophical that the New-Critical task of divorcing the writer from his work seems, in this case, to entail more trouble than it is worth. See James McConkey, *The Novels of E. M. Forster* (Ithaca, 1957), pp. 2-5, 86.

[4] Stephen Spender, *World Within World* (London, 1951), p. 167.

within the frame of nineteenth-century liberalism and humanism, and their real originality lies only in their refinement upon
that body of thought. It would seem necessary, if we are to
avoid misconstruing Forster as either an eccentric or an anti-
quarian, to recall and examine the formative influences on his
intellectual life. Beneath his diffident exterior we shall find a
rigorous and consistent thinker who has defined his beliefs in
terms of the basic issues of Victorian controversy—issues that
are now unfashionable but by no means dead. Indeed, Forster's
ability to assimilate or ignore change deserves to be seen, not as
a failure of alertness or flexibility, but as evidence of the thor-
oughness and conviction in his early critique of Victorianism.
His serenity is that of a man who has found that his education
has on the whole provided him with a wider outlook than any
contained in the fanaticisms of the following age.

In stressing Forster's consistency, however, I do not mean to
imply that his career shows no development at all. Though he
has maintained a steady front toward the outside world, he
seems to have been increasingly responsive to the implications of
his own philosophy. I am thinking of Forster's whole position as
a humanist—as a man who places his faith in this world and
who takes the individual human norm as the measure of everything. In theory Forster remains loyal to this position throughout his career, but as a novelist he finds himself drawn more and
more to its negative side. We shall repeatedly be faced with the
inference that Forster's artistic growth runs parallel to his progressive embracing of the ironies and disappointments inherent
in humanism. The acceptance of the perils of humanism becomes, indeed, a major touchstone of value in his novels and
finally emerges as his dominant theme. This phenomenon is the
real object of our interest, and we shall look at it from various
sides. First, however, we must define Forster's humanism more
fully and locate its historical sources.

Two

FORSTER AND RELIGION: FROM
CLAPHAM TO BLOOMSBURY

The importance of religious questions in E. M. Forster's novels, though easy to underestimate, is impossible to neglect entirely. Even *Where Angels Fear to Tread* and *A Room with a View* are influenced, however discreetly, by convictions about the meaning of life, and this is more obviously true of *The Longest Journey*, *Howards End*, and *A Passage to India*. Yet Forster's anti-clericalism and his light regard for Christian theology can give a one-sided view of his religious position. Everyone knows that he is an agnostic, but his agnosticism is complicated by romantic evasions, by what we might call a thwarted fascination with the Absolute.

Though Forster's temperament is ultimately responsible for his balance of attitudes, their range was limited by his background. Forster himself is the first to recognize this; his slant on life, he has said, was "derived from the Thorntons,"[1] his father's family. He adds, to be sure, that this slant was altered by later influences, and we shall examine some of these in subsequent chapters. Meanwhile, however, we can understand the main source of Forster's agnosticism by seeing its emergence from a family and class tradition.

Forster traces his ancestry to a particular branch of what Noël Annan has called the "intellectual aristocracy" of the British upper middle class.[2] His grandfather, the Reverend Charles

[1] E. M. Forster, *Marianne Thornton: A Domestic Biography 1797-1887* (New York, 1956), pp. 301f.
[2] The incredible system of intermarriages that perpetuated this "aristocracy" is traced by Annan in *Leslie Stephen: His Thought and Character in Relation to His Time* (Cambridge, Mass., 1952), pp. 3f., and more

Forster, was a relatively poor Irish clergyman, but when he married Laura Thornton in 1833 he allied himself and his heirs with one of the most important families in the English Evangelical movement. Although Charles Forster and his son Edward did not belong to the "Clapham Sect," E. M. Forster regards that circle as his intellectual starting-place. This is because Marianne Thornton, Forster's paternal great-aunt, took a particular interest in him as a child, and because his mother, Alice Whichelo Forster, was herself a special protégée of Marianne from the age of twelve.[3] There was thus a connection with the Evangelical Thorntons on both sides of the family, and although Forster was still an infant when his father died, his mother, grandmother, and great-aunt perpetuated the Thornton influence.

The Clapham Sect, derisively named by Sydney Smith, was not really a religious sect but a group of wealthy and pious Anglicans, members of the upper bourgeoisie, who worked together to effect certain public reforms. Henry Thornton, Forster's great-grandfather, was the central figure; it was his house on Clapham Common that became the group's headquarters, and his money, energy, and skill in Parliament that gave the movement much of its original strength. The Sect agitated for sabbatarianism, the abolition of slavery, the encouragement of relief for the poor, the abolition of cruel games, prison reform, reform of the game laws, and the spread of missionary societies. More important than any of these, however, was the indirect influence of the Sect's moral fervor, which touched all shades of religious belief and helped to determine the character of Victorian philanthropy. Like other Evangelicals, the Clap-

---

fully in "The Intellectual Aristocracy," *Studies in Social History: a Tribute to G. M. Trevelyan*, ed. J. H. Plumb (London, New York, Toronto, 1955), pp. 243-287. It may suffice here to recall the names Arnold, Macaulay, Darwin, Huxley, Stephen, Trevelyan, Cornford, Berenson, and—with special reference to Bloomsbury—Bell, Woolf, Strachey, Smith, and Keynes.

[3] See *Marianne Thornton*, pp. 279-281.

hamites laid emphasis on the personal assurance of salvation and on daily meditation and self-criticism. Their social prominence, however, gave them a certain repose, almost an eclectic quality, that was decidedly atypical of Evangelicalism. Forster writes that Battersea Rise, Marianne Thornton's home, "was anything but a 'Victorian' establishment and . . . charges of narrowness and stuffiness must be brought against it with caution. It appears, rather, as a blend of feudal loyalty and eighteenth-century enlightenment. . . ." (*Marianne Thornton*, p. 26) Of the Thorntons' religion he says approvingly: "The power of the Church over the Thorntons was moral rather than mystic. They were indifferent to ceremony, their references to Holy Communion are temperate, and though they desired sound doctrine they were not upset by deviations from it." (*Ibid.*, p. 32) And in an essay reprinted in *Two Cheers for Democracy*, Forster admits that Henry Thornton's solid character is not "inspiring" to the restless modern mind and that the Thornton family prayers have no meaning for us, but he does not conceal his admiration for his ancestors' good sense, good taste, and dedication to good works.

Only on two points does Forster consider the Thorntons to have been narrow-minded. One charge, that they were indifferent to the evils of the industrial system to which they owed their vast power, will be taken up in the next chapter. Secondly, Forster gives us a brief but highly significant critique of the Thorntons' religion. The Clapham Sect, he says, was too easily led to reduce spiritual matters to the commonplace terms of daily life. Quakers, on the other hand, "have what the Claphamites lacked: a touch of mysticism, a sense of the unseen, and a capacity for martyrdom." Forster continues: "These impulses, whatever their objective value, do purge the soul, in a way which alms-giving and self-examination cannot; they do lift the participant into a region outside money, whereas charity only keeps man running to and fro, from his business to his deserving cause, and then back to his business. . . . This indifference to the unseen seems to me the great defect in my great-grandfather's set, and the reason why they have not made a bigger name in history. It came out in everything—in the books they collected, in the letters my great-aunts wrote to one another, and in the comments which they made upon life, which are surprisingly dry for people so pious. Poetry, mystery, passion, ecstasy, music, don't count."[4]

In one sense this is a detached and casual estimate; Forster is little concerned with choosing among competing forms of Christianity. But "poetry, mystery, passion, ecstasy, music" express Forster's own strain of religiosity if not of religion, and it is important to him that these things are missing from his family heritage. He can share the Thorntons' temperance of manner, but he has never thought of restricting his spiritual horizon to theirs.

If we pursue the "intellectual aristocracy" beyond the first two generations, however, we arrive at an atmosphere more pertinent to Forster. The Bloomsbury Group, Forster's circle of acquaintance in Cambridge and London, consisted entirely of this class, and formulated its values with deliberate reference to those of the previous, largely agnostic generation. The skepticism of Forster and his friends came not from personal experiences of disillusion but from a legacy which they accepted with varying degrees of earnestness.

To see Forster's views in historical relief, therefore, we may examine those of the most famous "parent" of Bloomsbury, Leslie Stephen.[5] Like Forster, he was linked to Clapham on both sides of his family.[6] The household of his father, Sir James

---

[4] *Two Cheers for Democracy* (New York, 1951), p. 195.

[5] Editor of the first twenty-six volumes of the *Dictionary of National Biography*, Stephen was author of the *History of English Thought in the Eighteenth Century, The English Utilitarians, The Science of Ethics, English Literature and Society in the Eighteenth Century,* and numerous biographies. He was also, of course, the father of Virginia Woolf and Vanessa Bell.

[6] Stephen's two grandfathers were the Rev. John Venn, Rector of Clapham, and James Stephen, an influential Claphamite.

Stephen, was typical of Clapham's second generation in the mildness of its religious atmosphere. The bulk of emphasis was laid, not upon dogmatic moral rules and the moment of conversion, but on a general sense of duty. At Cambridge, though he was obliged to take Holy Orders to qualify for a fellowship, Stephen read widely in the secular philosophers and did not hesitate to befriend irreligious and radical dons such as Henry Fawcett. When his religious crisis came, it was naturally less severe than those of Carlyle and Newman; indeed, it was hardly a crisis at all. He wrote of his conversion to agnosticism: "In truth, I did not feel that the solid ground was giving way beneath my feet, but rather that I was being relieved of a cumbrous burden. I was not discovering that my creed was false, but that I had never really believed it."[7]

Stephen's belief in scientific empiricism led him to view the paradoxes of religion as contradictions that proved the system invalid. In "An Agnostic's Apology" he concludes that philosophical speculation is fruitless. The standard difficulties of Christian theology, such as the problems of free will and of the relationship between the orders of nature and grace, are, he says, questions of fact. "Questions of fact can only be solved by examining facts,"[8] and theologians cannot even agree on what facts there are to examine. Who is to decide which revelation is the true one? "The only appeal is to experience, and to appeal to experience is to admit the fundamental dogma of Agnosticism."[9] Having thus bound theology helplessly to matter, Stephen turns with approval to science—the one reliable

---

[7] Leslie Stephen, *Some Early Impressions* (London, 1924), p. 70. This is not to say, of course, that Stephen's generation was altogether happy with its disbelief. The words of W. K. Clifford, Stephen's contemporary, suggest a different mood: "We have seen the spring sun shine out of an empty heaven, to light up a soulless earth: we have felt with utter loneliness that the Great Companion is dead"; from "The Influence upon Morality of a Decline in Religious Belief," *The Ethics of Belief; and Other Essays* (London, 1947), p. 124.

[8] Leslie Stephen, *An Agnostic's Apology; and Other Essays* (London, 1903), p. 38.

[9] *ibid.*, p. 39.

11

tool for interpreting the knowable world. Science, he argues, does not take us far, but it shows us the limits of our intelligence and guards us against error: "Here we shall find sufficient guidance for the needs of life, though we renounce for ever the attempt to get behind the veil which no one has succeeded in raising; if, indeed, there be anything behind."[10]

Like the Utilitarians who preceded him, Stephen not only undermined the traditional grounds of moral judgment, but attempted to introduce a "science" of morality in their place. The laws governing the health of the social organism were to be discovered inductively, and to state them would be to lay down the moral code.[11] Here we have no melancholy retreat from religious issues, but a confidence that the Christian system can be surpassed. In practice Stephen retains Christian morality almost intact, but his subjection of it to "scientific" tests of legitimacy is a portentous deviation from the attitude of his forebears.

The historical significance of Stephen's ideas lies more in their typicality than in their novelty. Stephen himself regarded his work as derivative; he acknowledged his ethical system to be an outgrowth of John Stuart Mill's theories as modified by Darwin and Spencer.[12] Many of Stephen's contemporaries, moreover, were engaged in constructing the same kind of agnostic synthesis as his own. Huxley, Spencer, John Tyndall, W. K. Clifford, and John Morley shared Stephen's faith that science could replace Christianity, and many third-generation Claphamites, such as John Venn, A. V. Dicey, Sir G. O. Trevelyan, and Stephen's brother Fitzjames, concurred to the extent of ceasing to look for intellectual certainty in Christianity.[13] Stephen's attack on theology may have been more purposeful than those of his friends, but it failed to shock or surprise any-

[10] *ibid.*, p. 40.
[11] See "The Scepticism of Believers," *ibid.*, pp. 71f.
[12] Leslie Stephen, *The Science of Ethics* (London, 1882), Preface, pp. *v-vii.*
[13] See Annan, *Leslie Stephen,* p. 122.

one; it was merely the articulation of a feeling that had become more or less general.

If we now return to Forster we can see the effects of still further removal from Clapham. There is, of course, no reason to suppose that all the differences between Forster and Stephen are culturally meaningful, but it would be equally mistaken to attribute everything to personalities. Forster describes himself frankly as "a child of unbelief." (*Abinger Harvest*, p. 100) Elsewhere he explains that the very idea of religious belief offends him: "I do not believe in Belief. . . . Faith, to my mind, is a stiffening process, a sort of mental starch, which ought to be applied as sparingly as possible. I dislike the stuff. I do not believe in it, for its own sake, at all. Herein I probably differ from most people, who believe in Belief, and are only sorry they cannot swallow even more than they do. My law-givers are Erasmus and Montaigne, not Moses and St. Paul. My temple stands not upon Mount Moriah but in that Elysian Field where even the immoral are admitted. My motto is: 'Lord, I disbelieve—help thou my unbelief.'" (*Two Cheers*, p. 67)

This is an attitude quite different in its ease and wryness from the militant tone of Leslie Stephen. Yet Forster's basic reasoning is really akin to Stephen's. He is convinced, as Stephen was, that dogmatism shuts out the real complexity of things. His essays repeatedly assert that truth is evasive and only to be seized in fragments. "The human mind," he has said, "is not a dignified organ, and I do not see how we can exercise it sincerely except through eclecticism."[14] Or again: "There is no such person as a philosopher; no one is detached; the observer, like the observed, is in chains." (*Two Cheers*, p. 10) With this outlook Forster necessarily denies himself the hope of seeing life both steadily and whole; he would prefer to see it steadily and to admit the incompleteness of his conclusions. The only subject on which he is dogmatic, in fact, is that of man's innate limitations: "We cannot understand each other, except in a rough and ready way;

[14] *Aspects of the Novel* (New York, 1927), p. 212.

we cannot reveal ourselves, even when we want to; what we call intimacy is only a makeshift; perfect knowledge is an illusion." (*Aspects of the Novel*, p. 98)

This unusually low opinion of human faculties gives a pessimistic cast to Forster's rationalism. While he agrees with Stephen in rejecting authority and distrusting intuition, his belief in reason is less vigorous than Stephen's. Whereas Stephen thought of science virtually as a substitute for religion, Forster has seen it allied to the technology of war and thought-control. Nor does he follow Stephen in assuming that, because our knowledge cannot penetrate "beyond the veil" of the tangible world, there may not be anything beyond at all. He is obsessed with the idea that life has some significance we cannot quite grasp—some pattern, perhaps a cruel one, which draws together things that analysis would never connect.

Forster's sense of mystery, indeed, seems to be closely related to his sense of artistic value. He can say unblushingly of Van Gogh, as Leslie Stephen would never have said of anyone: "He has a home beyond comfort and common sense with the saints, and perhaps he sees God." (*Two Cheers*, p. 6) He can say approvingly of Ibsen that "his stage throbs with a mysteriousness for which no obvious preparation has been made, with beckonings, tremblings, sudden compressions of the air, and his characters as they wrangle among the oval tables and stoves are watched by an unseen power which slips between their words." (*Abinger Harvest*, p. 86) In Forster's own writing this sense of elusive meaning governs the exploitation of fantasy and surprise; his characters, who are never quite in control of their destiny, are forcibly reminded that their mental equipment is imperfect.

Forster, we may say, has a theological preoccupation without a theology to satisfy it. Unlike Stephen and his freethinking comrades, who thought they needed only to erase superstition in order to achieve moral progress, he seems haunted by a feeling of ultimate despair. This is best illustrated in a strange, brief

14

essay of 1919 entitled "The Game of Life." Life, Forster says, is reluctant to explain her meaning to us, but schoolmasters and moralists will tell us readily that life is a game: "They love discussing what we ought to be instead of what we have to face—reams about conduct and nothing about those agitating apparitions that rise from the ground or fall from the sky." (*Ibid.*, p. 58) Nevertheless, the analogy of a game has some appropriateness, for life gives the illusion of producing winners and losers, successes and failures. Yet it is illusion and nothing more; life "has evolved the imposing doctrine of effort and reward to obscure her purposelessness. . . ." (*Ibid.*, p. 58) And men are dimly aware of this truth, for their actual games fail to gratify them. Victory always seems shallow, while loss suggests "nasty infinities" of correspondence with our ultimate fate. (*Ibid.*, p. 58).

Forster's concern is thus not with "the rules of the game," but with the alarming thought that our playing fairly or unfairly will probably not affect the predetermined outcome. He elaborates this idea with grim humor in the concluding paragraph of the essay, after he has facetiously decided that the best image of life is provided by piquet. "It is in the first place obviously and overwhelmingly unfair. Fate is dealt, despite skill in discarding, and neither in the rules of play nor in the marking is there the least attempt to redress misfortune or to give the sufferer a fresh chance. The bias is all the other way. Disaster is an additional reason for disaster—culminating in the crowning butchery of Rubicon, where the very bones of the victim are gathered up by the conqueror and flung like sticks upon his bonfire. Yet this savage pastime admits the element of Free Will. It is possible to retard or accelerate Fate. Play, subtle and vigorous play, goes on all the time, though the player is being swept to disaster or victory by causes beyond his control, and it is in the play, rather than the result, that the real interest of the game resides. Another affair, in which all the living and possibly all the dead are engaged, runs on similar lines. Failure or success seem to have been allotted to men by their stars. But they retain the power of wriggling, of fighting with their star or against it, and in the whole universe the only really interesting movement is this wriggle." (*Ibid.*, pp. 59f.)

"The Game of Life" is exceptional in its bitter sarcasm, but it does not misrepresent Forster's ideas about fate as we can gather them from his other writings. It is not too much to say that the imagination of disaster—the perception of Matthew Arnold's "something that infects the world"—is the necesary condition of Forster's detached irony. His scorn for human illusions sets him apart from all notions of success or salvation. Though he sees beauty in W. H. Auden's dream of an ideally Christian civilization, for example, he feels compelled to add: "For some of us who are non-Christian there still remains the comfort of the non-human, the relief, when we look up at the stars, of realising that they are uninhabitable." (*Two Cheers*, p. 268) It is as if Forster were consoling himself here with a kind of inverted Calvinism, an assurance that neither he nor anyone else is among the saved.

It is this somewhat morbid feeling of neglect that most clearly separates Forster's attitude from Leslie Stephen's. Stephen and his friends turned to agnosticism because they found Christianity unconvincing as a version of history and incomplete as a moral system. Forster would reject Christianity, if for no other reason, simply because it *is* a moral system. He is more concerned with "those agitating apparitions that rise from the ground or fall from the sky" than with justifying man's right to God's attention. If our philosophy is, as William James proposed, "our individual way of just seeing and feeling the total push and pressure of the cosmos,"[15] we can say that Forster's philosophy is a more *oppressed* one than Leslie Stephen's. He has a sense of transcendent reality, but the reality he envisions is a universe almost lifeless, almost empty, and wholly devoid of respect for the hu-

[15] William James, *Pragmatism; and Four Essays from The Meaning of Truth* (New York, 1959), p. 18.

man. "The disintegrating sea, the twisted sky"[16] constitute the metaphysical backdrop for his thoughts.

There are, of course, additional reasons for Forster's disapproval of Christianity. Fanaticism of all kinds is repugnant to him, and he does not distinguish between Christianity in general and the fanaticism of the ascetic saints. Christians, according to Forster, believe in "wearing away the body by penance, in order that the quivering soul may be exposed"; but his own motto, derived from his notion of Hellenic reasonableness, is "cherish the body and you will cherish the soul." (*Abinger Harvest*, p. 172) Like Gibbon, he looks upon the advent of Christianity as a major catastrophe for civilization, a senseless and small-minded vengeance against the Greek ideal. The comparison is not random; Gibbon is Forster's favorite historian,[17] and his own treatment of history has a Gibbonesque urbanity. In *Pharos and Pharillon*, a collection of essays on Alexandria, he repeatedly asserts that Christianity barbarized the areas it conquered, and that it was able to thrive only "where the antique civilization had failed to make men dignified."[18] A good part of the book is taken up with sardonic accounts of theological quarreling within the early Church, and the emphasis is laid in every case upon the triumph of monomania, hypocrisy, and antihumanism. As for Christianity's persistent influence in the modern world, this, says Forster elsewhere, must be "due to the money behind it, rather than to its spiritual appeal." (*Two Cheers*, pp. 75f.)

The offhand manner of this dismissal calls to mind the early attitude of John Maynard Keynes, who in his Bloomsbury days regarded Christianity as mere "hocus-pocus."[19] Or, better yet, it may remind us of the young Lytton Strachey, who is said to have given up the idea of writing a life of Jesus because, he ex-

---

[16] *The Collected Tales of E. M. Forster* (New York, 1947), Introduction, p. *viii*.

[17] See *Abinger Harvest*, pp. 218-225, and *Two Cheers*, pp. 162-166, 304.

[18] *Pharos and Pharillon* (New York, 1923), p. 51.

[19] John Maynard Keynes, *Two Memoirs; Dr. Melchior: A Defeated Enemy, and My Early Beliefs* (London, 1949), p. 96.

plained, no evidence could be found for the existence of such a personage.[20] The third, or Bloomsbury, generation of Clapham's descendants was raised in ignorance of theology, and affected to look back on the Christian age with Voltairean amusement. In his passages of satire Forster is altogether typical of the Bloomsbury spirit.

It is clear, however, that to take Forster only in his satirical mood is to remain on the surface. His wit, perhaps like all wit, is a means of coping with dissatisfaction, a compromise with misgivings that refuse to vanish. Forster's religious misgivings are stated plainly enough in "The Game of Life," but, more importantly, they lurk behind each of his novels and finally step forward to assume control in A *Passage to India*.

[20] See R. F. Harrod, *The Life of John Maynard Keynes* (London, 1951), p. 84.

Three

THE REFUGE OF LIBERALISM

The relevance of Forster's political views to his novels is far from obvious. Of the novels, only *Howards End* and *A Passage to India* have to do with politics, and these are anything but partisan tracts. The theme of *Howards End* is the need not for reform but for broad compromises between men and women, innovation and tradition, intellect and action, the upper classes and the lower. *A Passage to India* moves still farther beyond a simple creed or platform. It suggests that we are doomed by our nature to ignorance of God and isolation from one another—that not prayer nor politics nor social intercourse will save us from this fate. Such a Homeric perspective dwarfs the gestures of anti-imperialism that Forster does occasionally make in the novel. Personal political sentiments cannot seem very urgent in a book about the vanity of human wishes.

In a refined sense, however, it is possible to see considerable political meaning in Forster's novels. Their very lack of overt partisanship is consistent with his version of liberalism, which we can identify as a narrow but by no means private current within the wider liberal tradition. Forster's nonfiction leaves no doubt as to the centrality of political beliefs in his moral framework, and the novels reflect his deepest and most generalized thoughts on the subject. Indeed, the very existence of his novels has political interest if we consider them as a part of cultural history. Trained in the moral absolutes of a Liberal Party which lost both its power and its integrity while they were undergraduates, many of the Cambridge "intellectual aristocrats" of Forster's generation found in art the satisfaction their fathers had found in public life. It is not surprising to learn that Forster's

19

novels are conceived in terms of moral generalizations whose ultimate source is the political philosophy of liberalism.

Forster's unwillingness to be a party man has been evident throughout his career, even in his occasional sallies into political journalism. These have been provoked rather by indignation at abuses of power than by sympathy with the powerful. A typical piece from the postwar era is his poem, "A Voter's Dilemma," which explains in acid couplets that Liberals and Conservatives alike are more concerned with munitions profiteering than with peace and justice. (see *Abinger Harvest*, p. 31) From time to time Forster has lent his services to the British government, but always in the character of a moralist. His Labour Research Department pamphlet, "The Government of Egypt" (1920), for example, is a biting review of colonial policy, written out of an instinctive sympathy for the underdog. When in 1939 he served on the Lord Chancellor's committee to review the Law of Defamatory Libel, he was acting upon his lifelong hatred of censorship. Even his anti-Nazi essays and radio broadcasts during the Second World War bear the stamp of his unwillingness to indulge in political simplifications. While denouncing abuses of liberty in Germany he repeatedly turns back to England and cautions against the same abuses: "Not the beam in Dr. Goebbels' eye, but the mote in our own eye. Can we take it out? Is there as much freedom of expression and publication in this country as there might be?" (*Two Cheers*, p. 55)

Though they come late in his career, Forster's pronouncements on the twentieth century's various orthodoxies can give us a more specific idea of his political reasoning. Fascism he finds utterly unthinkable: "Fascism does evil that evil may come." (*Abinger Harvest*, p. 64) Because of his distaste for "the chaos and carnage of international finance" (*Two Cheers*, p. 7), he has praised the Communists for their effort to find something better. Communism, however, is too bloody in its methods of reform (see *Abinger Harvest*, pp. 64f., 76), and Stalinist Russia is a very imperfect Utopia. Forster is even suspicious of the mildest of collectivist movements, English Fabianism, on the grounds that it is latently autocratic. "Our danger from Fascism," he wrote in 1935, "—unless a war starts when anything may happen —is negligible. We're menaced by something much more insidious—by what I might call 'Fabio-Fascism,' by the dictator-spirit working quietly away behind the façade of constitutional forms, passing a little law (like the Sedition Act) here, endorsing a departmental tyranny there, emphasizing the national need of secrecy elsewhere, and whispering and cooing the so-called 'news' every evening over the wireless, until opposition is tamed and gulled." (*Ibid.*, pp. 65f.) While he has high praise for Beatrice and Sidney Webb and for Edward Carpenter (*Two Cheers*, pp. 212-218), Forster refuses to commit himself to socialism or to become sentimental over the plight of the working class.[1]

Behind all these judgments lies an uncompromising individualism. Governments are good or bad, for Forster, strictly according to their tolerance of variety and criticism; this is the basis for his grudging "two cheers" for British constitutional democracy. As for the positive achievements that a state might reach under one system or another, Forster counts them as nothing against the dangers that go along with governmental strength. If he is vaguely leftist in his sympathies, he is opposed in principle to the concentration of power that leftist programs require. He can agree, for instance, that housing must be found for London workers, but he cannot approve of commandeering a "satellite town" for them in the uprooted countryside of his own home country: ". . . I cannot equate the problem. It is a collision of loyalties. I cannot free myself from the conviction that something irreplaceable has been destroyed, and that a little piece of England has died as surely as if a bomb had hit it." (*Two Cheers*, p. 59) Forster's respect for the countryside, the last fortress of individualism in a world of urban sameness, overrides his concern for the material benefit of the majority.

---

[1] See, e.g., *Goldsworthy Lowes Dickinson* (London, 1934), p. 87.

Ultimately we may say that it is Forster's disbelief in the discrete reality of the state that checks his socialism. He sees the nation, not as an entity in itself with international interests to be protected, but simply as a sum total of individual citizens. To "make sacrifices for the state" is thus to trick oneself with words.[2] Occasionally Forster has tried to define a ground where national programs are possible—"We want planning for the body and not for the spirit" (*Two Cheers*, p. 57)—but in reality he can observe no such distinction. As a nominalist and a moralist he is forever afraid of the arbitrariness, the impersonality, and the blindness of group-power. "The more highly public life is organised," he writes, "the lower does its morality sink." (*Ibid.*, p. 74)

In this light it is hardly surprising that Forster has looked with increasing horror and despair upon the twentieth century's tendency to spawn dictatorships and superstates. In his best-known essay, "What I Believe," after explaining that he disbelieves in belief, gives only two cheers for democracy, and is solaced in the modern world only by friendship and art, he concludes: "The above are the reflections of an individualist and a liberal who has found liberalism crumbling beneath him and at first felt ashamed. Then, looking around, he decided there was no special reason for shame, since other people, whatever they felt, were equally insecure. And as for individualism—there seems no way of getting off this, even if one wanted to. The dictator-hero can grind down his citizens till they are all alike, but he cannot melt them into a single man. That is beyond his power. He can order them to merge, he can incite them to mass-

[2] In this connection see especially "The Menace to Freedom," *Two Cheers*, p. 10: "Man has dallied with the idea of a social conscience, and has disguised the fear of the herd as loyalty towards the group, and has persuaded himself that when he sacrifices himself to the State he is accomplishing a deed far more satisfying than anything which can be accomplished alone. Alone? As if he had ever been alone! He has never had the opportunity. Only Heaven knows what Man might accomplish alone! The service that is perfect freedom, perhaps."

antics, but they are obliged to be born separately, and to die separately, and, owing to these unavoidable termini, will always be running off the totalitarian rails. The memory of birth and the expectation of death always lurk within the human being, making him separate from his fellows and consequently capable of intercourse with them. Naked I came into the world, naked I shall go out of it! And a very good thing too, for it reminds me that I am naked under my shirt, whatever its colour." (*Ibid.*, p. 76)[3]

Here is rear-guard action of the least hopeful sort. Forster has conceded the political field to the dictator-hero; liberalism will not survive, and individualism can be nearly exterminated in the name of federal authority. "The memory of birth and the expectation of death" will hardly prove adequate consolation when Big Brother has finished his work of molding the ideal citizen, and Forster is understandably reluctant to play an active role in a world heading this way. "We who seek the truth," as he rather dramatically wrote in 1923, "are only concerned with politics when they deflect us from it." (*Abinger Harvest*, p. 269)[4]

The liberalism evident here would seem to be far removed from the politics of the Liberal Party or of any party, but this is not wholly true. Forster himself recognizes his debt to the tradition of nineteenth-century liberalism, and in one important passage he explains where he agrees and disagrees with his forebears: "I belong to the fag-end of Victorian liberalism, and can look back to an age whose challenges were moderate in their

[3] One is reminded here of Freud's answer to the charge that he was neither a Fascist nor a Communist, neither black nor red. "No," he replied, "one should be flesh coloured." Quoted by Ernest Jones, *The Life and Work of Sigmund Freud*, Vol. III (New York, 1957), p. 343. Freud, incidentally, took his politics directly from John Stuart Mill.

[4] A fuller statement appears in a letter, dated January 13, 1958, to the present writer: "I have never belonged to any political party, and have only become interested in public affairs when the community appeared to be oppressing the individual, or when one community appeared to be oppressing another." (Quoted with Mr. Forster's permission.)

tone, and the cloud on whose horizon was no bigger than a man's hand. In many ways it was an admirable age. It practised benevolence and philanthropy, was humane and intellectually curious, upheld free speech, had little colour-prejudice, believed that individuals are and should be different, and entertained a sincere faith in the progress of society. The world was to become better and better, chiefly through the spread of parliamentary institutions. The education I received in those far-off and fantastic days made me soft and I am very glad it did, for I have seen plenty of hardness since, and I know it does not even pay. . . . But though the education was humane it was imperfect, inasmuch as we none of us realised our economic position. In came the nice fat dividends, up rose the lofty thoughts, and we did not realise that all the time we were exploiting the poor of our own country and the backward races abroad, and getting bigger profits from our investments than we should. We refused to face this unpalatable truth." (*Two Cheers*, p. 56)

The notion of Victorian liberalism projected here accords well with Lionel Trilling's account of the liberal tradition as "that loose body of middle class opinion which includes such ideas as progress, collectivism and humanitarianism."[5] To be historically scrupulous, however, one would have to point out that Trilling's definition is incomplete and even confused. Collectivism and humanitarianism were once recognized as very antitheses of liberal doctrine. Forster's paragraph refers not to liberalism as a movement but to the practice of a minority of liberals, the descendants of Clapham, whose "benevolence and philanthropy" derived rather from their religion than from their politics. Forster is aligning himself only with those liberals who have rejected *laissez faire* economics while preserving and reinterpreting the liberal ideal of individualism.

Forster's offshoot of liberalism had developed chiefly from

[5] Lionel Trilling, *E. M. Forster* (London, 1944), p. 13.

John Stuart Mill's critique of Jeremy Bentham. Through most of the nineteenth century the word "liberalism" was considered synonymous with Utilitarianism or philosophic radicalism, the economic theory of Adam Smith, Malthus, Ricardo, Bentham, and James Mill. At midcentury, when the younger Mill was supplanting his father and Bentham as the leading radical theorist, Utilitarianism was little more than the articulation of middle-class capitalist interests. Its calculus of value according to "the greatest happiness of the greatest number" was in practice a rationale for free trade, economic expansionism, and democratic government. Utilitarians favored individualism, but only in the business sense of the word; they recognized no intrinsic rights of individuals for protection against the majority will. It was only because the Utilitarians happened to concur with Rights-of-Man liberals in opposing the landed aristocracy and supporting middle-class suffrage that radical economists found themselves led, in Halévy's words, "to confound economic liberalism with moral liberalism."[6]

This confusion of liberalisms, which widely persisted until Forster's day and of which the Bloomsbury group was sharply aware, was the central issue in Mill's quarrel with his father's generation of radicals. Though he always considered himself a loyal Benthamite, Mill set out, as he later explained, "to show that there was a Radical philosophy, better and more complete than Bentham's, while recognizing and incorporating all of Bentham's which is permanently valuable."[7] He felt that Bentham had oversimplified human nature in assuming all pleasures and pains to be qualitatively equal; because of man's involvement with moral and religious sanctions, Mill argued, happiness cannot be gauged by statistics of production and consumption. In politics, too, Mill tempered Bentham's faith in democracy. While previous Utilitarians had felt that the government should

[6] Elie Halévy, *The Growth of Philosophic Radicalism*, tr. Mary Morris (London, 1934), p. 117.
[7] John Stuart Mill, *Autobiography* (New York, 1948), p. 150.

swiftly enact the majority's wishes into law, Mill saw the long-range value of constitutional restraints. The Utilitarian principle, once freed from a purely economic definition of welfare, demanded that dissenters be protected. Society could not afford to stamp out the vital minority whose unpopular views might later turn out to be indispensable.

Mill's reasoning is founded on a nominalism very similar to Forster's. His concern is not with defining the sacrifices we owe to the state, but with establishing "a limit to the legitimate interference of collective opinion with individual independence."[8] Again, a love of diversity is crucial in both writers. The power of the majority, for Mill, is valuable only so far as it is "tempered by respect for the personality of the individual, and deference to superiority of cultivated intelligence."[9] Forster, living in a later age, is concerned about the likelihood that this respect for individuality will be overridden by Benthamite planners. Such men, he says, "assure us that the new economy will evolve an appropriate morality, and that when all people are properly fed and housed, they will have an outlook which will be right, because they are the people. I cannot swallow that. I have no mystic faith in the people. I have in the individual. He seems to me a divine achievement and I mistrust any view which belittles him." (*Two Cheers*, p. 57)

If Forster's preference for *laissez faire* in the world of the spirit goes back to Mill, so too does his rejection of *laissez faire* in the economic world (see *Ibid.*, p. 57). Though he always supported free trade, Mill eventually turned the Utilitarian principle against the prejudices of its founders. By the end of his career he was openly considering the possibility that socialism may be the expression of man's highest political goals.[10] The ulti-

[8] John Stuart Mill, "On Liberty," *Utilitarianism, Liberty, and Representative Government* (London, 1931), p. 68.

[9] *Mill on Bentham and Coleridge*, ed. F. R. Leavis (London, 1950), p. 88. See also the epigraph to "On Liberty," which proclaims "the absolute and essential importance of human development in its richest diversity."

[10] See Michael St. John Packe, *The Life of John Stuart Mill* (London, 1954), pp. 310-314.

mate social problem, he and his wife decided, was "how to unite the greatest individual liberty of action, with a common owner-ship in the raw material of the globe, and an equal participation of all in the benefits of combined labour."[11]

This coincidence of liberal individualism with what English-men called "progressivism" and Americans "radicalism" has enabled Mill to be a kind of patron saint for two widely dif-ferent groups. Progressives such as Henry Fawcett, the Webbs, Shaw, and Wells could look to Mill as a theorist of the most sweeping reform of society. These men were opposed to *laissez faire*, but their own politics belong in the Benthamite tradition of serving the greatest-happiness principle at the expense of existing institutions. It is the Benthamite side of Mill that has nourished English socialism. Mill's defense of private liberty, on the other hand, points toward the nonpolitical liberalism that we see in Forster. The liberalism of Walter Bagehot and T. H. Green, and more pertinently of Matthew Arnold and Samuel Butler, seems to belong to this tradition. Such a liberalism does not concern itself with adaptation to new economic and social conditions but with the protection of a fixed ideal of individual freedom. It fears the rule of the mob as well as the rule of the few, and tends finally to disengage itself from party loyalty.

These two divergent branches of liberalism existed side by side within the Liberal Party. Gladstone, the quintessential Liberal, illustrated in his own person the contradictory sources of the party's strength. A High-Church Tory at heart, a friend of private fortunes, and a believer in "the rule of the best," he neverthe-less became the spokesman for popular democracy, free trade, Catholic emancipation, reform of the Civil Service, and Irish Home Rule, all but the last of which were congenial to the spirit of Benthamism. Gladstone was anything but "progressive" in his moral outlook. His ambition was to render the morality of private life totally applicable to politics—in other words, to Christianize national policy. He supported repeal of the Corn

[11] *Autobiography*, p. 162.

Laws, for example, not as an economic reform but to satisfy a point of justice, and his campaign to alleviate poverty rose from a belief that greater material welfare would help to improve the nation's ethics. The distance between this kind of reasoning and the Utilitarian calculus is of course immense, but Gladstone's popularity, together with the concurrence of his policies with Benthamite programs, held the Liberal Party together until the 1890's.

The inconsistency and weakness of the Liberal Party in that decade undoubtedly helped to confirm E. M. Forster in his abstention from partisanship. The Liberals had always been composed of a rather uneasy coalition of Whigs, Radicals, and Peelites, who were united more by their opposition to Disraeli than by any common ground of philosophy. With Disraeli's death in 1881, the debacle of Khartoum in 1885, and the public identification of Gladstone with Home Rule and Parnellism after that year, the party began to disintegrate rapidly. Gladstone's second Home Rule defeat and retirement in 1894 left the party without a widely respected leader. And in the period 1899-1902, when most of the future Bloomsbury writers were undergraduates at Cambridge, the Liberals were further weakened by the divisive issue of the South African War.[12] Almost all the remaining Imperialists in the Liberal Party had gone over to the Conservatives by 1902. Leslie Stephen described what had become, in 1903, an impossible tangle of party lines: "The Radical takes credit for having transferred political power to the democracy, though the democracy sets at defiance the old Radical's hatred of Government interference and of all Socialistic legislation. The Tory boasts that the prejudice against State interference has vanished, though the rulers of the State have now to interfere as the servants and not as the masters of the democracy. Both sides have modified their creeds in the course

[12] See R. C. K. Ensor, "The Recession of Liberalism," *Ideas and Beliefs of the Victorians; An Historic Revaluation of the Victorian Age* (London, 1949), pp. 396-402.

of their flirtation with Socialism, till it is difficult to assign the true principle of either, or trace the affiliation of ideas."[13]

Where were liberals of the more idealistic stamp expected to turn? Exasperation with the Liberal Party had reached a point where disengagement and reassessment of principles were imperative. This was the case, for example, with the founders of the *Independent Review*, a journal whose principles we must now examine, for E. M. Forster "thought the new age had begun" (*Dickinson*, p. 116) when he read the first number, and himself became a contributor to later numbers. It is the *Independent Review* that suggests most clearly the connection between liberal politics and Forster's art.

One of this journal's founders was G. Lowes Dickinson, Forster's teacher and friend at Cambridge, whose biography Forster wrote in 1934. There Forster gives us a vivid idea of what the *Independent* promised for disenchanted young liberals of the day: "The first number appeared in October, 1903. Edward Jenks was the editor; Dickinson, F. W. Hirst, C. F. G. Masterman, G. M. Trevelyan and Wedd were the members of the editorial council; Roger Fry designed the cover. The main aim of the review was political. It was founded to combat the aggressive Imperialism and the protection campaign of Joe Chamberlain; and to advocate sanity in foreign affairs and a constructive policy at home. It was not so much a Liberal review as an appeal to Liberalism from the Left to be its better self—one of those appeals which have continued until the extinction of the Liberal party. Dickinson thus defends the opening number of his review against the free-lancing of Ashbee (Letter of November 11th, 1903): 'If Liberals as you say are not "constructive" that perhaps is due to the fact that they believe in Liberty which means that they think all legislation can do is to give the utmost scope to individuals to develop the best in them. That I confess is my own point of view. But I believe that to do that will mean gradual revolution of all the fundamentals of society,

[13] *Some Early Impressions*, pp. 81f.

law of property, law of contract, law of marriage. Yet all that revolution would be abortive unless people have ideals for which they individually care and which are of the spirit and not mere megalomania. . . .' "

Forster continues: ". . . 'The Independent Review' did not make much difference to the councils of the nation, but it struck a note which was new at that time, and had a great influence on a number of individuals—young people for the most part. We were being offered something which we wanted. Those who were Liberals felt that the heavy, stocky, body of their party was about to grow wings and leave the ground. Those who were not Liberals were equally filled with hope: they saw avenues opening into literature, philosophy, human relationships, and the road of the future passing through not insurmountable dangers to a possible Utopia. Can you imagine decency touched with poetry? It was thus that the 'Independent' appeared to us—a light rather than a fire, but a light that penetrated the emotions." (*Ibid.*, pp. 115f.)

Here, certainly, the tradition of Mill is unmistakable; Dickinson's statement that "all legislation can do is to give the utmost scope to individuals to develop the best in them" seems to come directly from *On Liberty*. Forster's perception of "avenues opening into literature, philosophy, human relationships" also reflects the liberal belief that a man's political principles should be a consistent extension of his entire moral life. It is noteworthy, too, that Dickinson's remarks align him with the late, "Utopian" Mill rather than with the young defender of *laissez faire*. He has reached Mill's idea that collectivist legislation is positively necessary to prevent society from exercising a tyranny of fortune and opinion over the individual.

Although Forster's contributions to the *Independent* were not political,[14] the fact that he eagerly submitted short stories

[14] Only two of those contributions (the ninth and tenth in the following list) remain uncollected. The complete list follows:
"Macolnia Shops," I (1903), 311-313; "Cnidus," II (1904), 278-282;

and "cultural" essays reflects his admiration for the editors' point of view. We need not assume that he was well versed in the complex problems of trade and Empire that were debated in the review by such experts as Jenks, Masterman, and Trevelyan. It is more likely that his Cambridge years had predisposed him to a general sympathy with the liberalism of Arnold and the later Mill. If he was not exercised by all the collectivist reforms demanded by the *Independent*, he must certainly have approved of its repeated emphasis on freedom of discussion, equality of opportunity, and the importance of the individual man.

One article, the unsigned editorial (probably by Jenks) in the opening number, will have to serve us as a sample of the *Independent's* political attitude. The author begins by castigating the Liberal Party for its confusion of *laissez faire* with human liberty in general, and suggests that the future lies with those who can draft collectivist laws to "ensure that individual enterprise is neither thwarted nor impaired, but merely guided into those channels in which it can produce its best results."[15] In a tone of visionary altruism he calls for three types of reform: a more equal distribution of income; readier means of education for everyone; and a strict governmental control over abuses of private wealth. All three of these proposals had been anticipated by Mill. And when the author exhorts the Liberal Party to overcome its unwillingness "to combine the old freedom with the new demand for order,"[16] we may recall Forster's sentence: "We want the New Economy with the Old Morality." (*Two Cheers*, p. 57) The only real difference between the two statements is

---

"The Road from Colonus," iii (1904), 124-134; "The Story of a Panic," iii (1904), 453-472; "The Other Side of the Hedge," iv (1904), 297-301; "Cardan," v (1905), 365-374; "The Eternal Moment," vi (1905), 206-215, *ii.* 86-95, 211-223 (this vol. has two sets of pagination); "Gemistus Pletho," vii (1905), 211-223; "Rostock and Wismar," viii (1906), 332-335; "Literary Eccentrics; A Review," xi (1906), 105-110; and "The Celestial Omnibus," *The Albany Review* (N.S. of the *Independent*), i (1908), 459-475.

[15] *Independent Review*, i (1903), 4.
[16] *ibid.*, p. 6.

one of stress; the editors of the *Independent* are confident of the "old freedom" and are anxious to fulfill "the new demand for order," whereas Forster, writing later in the century, is afraid that demands for order will gradually put the old freedom out of mind.

The most suggestive essay in the *Independent*, for our purposes, is by a more familiar author, G. K. Chesterton. Though it is only peripherally linked to politics, it tells us a good deal about the climate of thinking among Forster's generation of liberals. The essay, entitled "The Poetic Quality in Liberalism," opens with a consideration of the unique freedom of literature. Chesterton finds that literature tends to absolve itself from the chances and limitations of real life in order to touch the Platonic essences of things. It is in this rescue of objects from "the tedium of law and the inevitable," says Chesterton, that literature expresses its antagonism to the spirit of science; "and it is in this that it comes nearest, again and again in human history, . . . to the spirit which we call Liberalism."[17] Chesterton explains that by "Liberalism" he does not mean the current imperialistic ideas of the Liberal Party. Nor does he mean the kind of opportunism that seeks to justify immoral policies by resort to scientific necessity. He is thinking of the liberal principles of the French Revolution, which, like art, literature, and religion, seek to remove man from "the tyranny of circumstance" and make him "sacred and separate."[18] True liberalism, for Chesterton, stands apart from utility and declares that men and nations have inherent rights that no one, however strong, can call into question.

In most ways, of course, Chesterton is very different from Forster; the vague Platonism, the sense of absolute right and wrong, and the air of holiness in his essay are un-Forsterian. Nor does Chesterton's later career suggest any underlying agreement with Forster's principles. Yet it remains true that Forster is

[17] *Independent Review*, v (1905), 56.
[18] *ibid.*, pp. 60, 61.

essentially a liberal of the sort described here. The hatred of expediency, the sympathy for the underdog, the opposition to imperialism, the fervent belief in private freedom are all recognizable. Neither Forster nor Chesterton is willing to say that nations are entitled to a moral license denied to individuals. To kill another nation is murder, and to abandon the old morality in order to meet new conditions is inadmissible.

Of particular interest is Chesterton's assertion that true liberalism is antiscientific. The Chestertonian liberal believes in freedom *because* it is not to be found in nature: "Because Time is the enemy of all his children," he says, ". . . therefore we will ring them with a ring of swords, and write for them an inviolable charter; because they are weak we will make them immortal, that they may be themselves . . . for, like all other things which are human and therefore divine, they must have the sense of everlasting life in order to live at all."[19] Forster's voice is less pompous, yet he too, we remember, has affirmed a "mystic faith" in the individual: "He seems to me a divine achievement and I mistrust any view which belittles him." And Forster, too, wants to sanctify the human condition by affording it more respect than it "naturally" commands. "The people I respect most," he writes, "behave as if they were immortal and as if society was eternal. Both assumptions are false: both of them must be accepted as true if we are to go on eating and working and loving, and are to keep open a few breathing holes for the human spirit." (*Two Cheers*, p. 71)[20] For Chesterton and Forster alike, the sense of man's actual smallness and instability strengthens the impulse to protect weak persons and nations from the tyranny of stronger ones—even if the stronger one should happen to be England.

In Forster's novels this combination of pessimism and idealism is rendered in terms of dialectical struggle. Forster's best characters yearn for sure knowledge and a sense of absolute or-

[19] *Independent Review*, v, 6of.
[20] Virtually the same statement occurs in *Abinger Harvest*, p. 70.

der; they would like to become "sacred and separate" from the chaos of nature. Forster's plots remind them, however, that they are very much involved in nature; all attempts to falsify their subjection to natural process end in catastrophe. There is thus a thread of tragic irony in Forster. The most sensitive characters, who feel a need for something higher than their own petty circumstances, are by consequence the characters most liable to disillusion. Their awareness of imperfection spurs them toward an impossible, yet heroic, effort to "see life steadily and see it whole, group in one vision its transitoriness and its eternal youth. . . ."[21]

Forster's valuation of art itself seems to spring from his ideal of rescuing something from nature. It is just the awareness of disorder and impermanence in the real world that impels Forster to stress the unique value of art. "Art is valuable," he writes, "not because it is educational (though it may be), not because it is recreative (though it may be), not because everyone enjoys it (for everybody does not), not even because it has to do with beauty. It is valuable because it has to do with order, and creates little worlds of its own, possessing internal harmony, in the bosom of this disordered planet." (*Two Cheers*, pp. 59f.)

Chesterton's belief that literature at its best is "essentially a liberation of types, persons, and things" from "the tedium of law and the inevitable" bears comparison with Forster's account of the power of words in a work of art: "It is their power to create not only atmosphere, but a world, which, while it lasts, seems more real and solid than this daily existence of pickpockets and trams. . . . We have entered a universe that only answers to its own laws, supports itself, internally coheres, and has a new standard of truth. . . . A poem is absolute. The world created by words exists neither in space nor time though it has semblances of both, it is eternal and indestructible. . . ." (*Ibid.*, pp. 81f.)

[21] *Howards End* (New York, 1954), p. 269. Note that Forster borrows Matthew Arnold's phrase to characterize his intellectual ideal.

We can, I think, go one step farther and see a causal link between Forster's dependence on the orderliness of art and his disaffiliation from the unmanageable world of politics. Forster himself has more than once implied that art is his substitute for imperfect political creeds. In an essay of 1934 he recalled his distrust of all the "isms" but Communism, and added: "those who are, like myself, too old for communism or too conscious of the blood to be shed before its problematic victory, turn to literature, because it is disinterested." (*Abinger Harvest*, p. 76)[22] Literature is "part of our armour" (*Ibid.*, p. 75), it consoles us for our lack of power over real events. And in a later essay, "Art for Art's Sake," he proclaimed that order is "something evolved from within, not something imposed from without; it is an internal stability, a vital harmony, and in the social and political category it has never existed except for the convenience of historians." (*Two Cheers*, p. 90) Where is order to be found? In religion, for some people; but for Forster, chiefly in art. Art "achieves something which has often been promised by society, but always delusively. Ancient Athens made a mess—but the *Antigone* stands up. Renaissance Rome made a mess—but the ceiling of the Sistine got painted. James I made a mess—but there was *Macbeth*. Louis XIV—but there was *Phèdre*." (*Ibid.*, p. 92) Art, therefore, "is the cry of a thousand sentinels, the echo from a thousand labyrinths; it is the lighthouse which cannot be hidden: *c'est le meilleur témoignage que nous puissions donner de notre dignité.*" (*Ibid.*, p. 92)

I do not mean to say, of course, that Forster suddenly abandoned politics for art when the Liberal Party lost its moral power. Following in Arnold's steps, he must have been somewhat detached from party loyalties from the first. We might remember, however, that such a detachment owes much to the politics of Mill. When Forster castigated the Liberal Party for being tied

---

[22] Again, the use of Arnold's terminology is significant. The passage, in fact, appears in an essay on the continuing relevance of Arnold in the modern world.

down to material interests, he was simply showing loyalty to his own more detached liberalism. "It is better to be a human being dissatisfied than a pig satisfied," Mill had written; "better to be Socrates dissatisfied than a fool satisfied."[23] In purging itself of moral inconsistencies, one segment of nineteenth-century liberalism broke free from the greatest-happiness principle and seized upon an ideal of individual self-cultivation that could find complete embodiment only in art—and Forster's art will prove to be both sustained and, in the last analysis, restricted by that ideal.

[23] "Utilitarianism," *Utilitarianism*, p. 9.

Four

CAMBRIDGE AND "THE GOOD"

To say that Forster is a liberal, an individualist, and an agnostic is to be about as systematic as Forster himself; he distrusts labels and categories but is willing to name his loyalties in a general way. More specifically, however, we have already taken note of certain values that might be called absolute "goods" for Forster: sincerity, art, private freedom, diversity. And to this list we may add two items of comparable importance, namely, Forster's belief in affectionate personal relations and his feeling for the English countryside and its traditions.[1]

A faith in love or friendship among individuals is Forster's avowed starting-place in his attempt to find a measure of order in the chaotic modern world. Forster would sooner betray his country than betray a friend, for friendship is essential "if one is not to make a mess of life." (*Two Cheers*, p. 68) There exists, he says, an aristocracy of the sensitive, the considerate, and the plucky whose members are more loyal to each other than to any organization: "Their temple, as one of them remarked, is the Holiness of the Heart's Affection, and their kingdom, though they never possess it, is the wide-open world." (*Ibid.*, p. 74)[2] In each of Forster's novels a contrast is established between classes or nations and individuals, and in each case the problem of the individuals is the same: to overcome the artificial barriers of status and reach out to find their true brothers. Though his characters are usually enmeshed in what they imagine to be social obligations, Forster himself feels that their primary duty is to be loyal to "the Heart's Affection," and in every case the

---

[1] We might also consider the pursuit of truth as a separate "good"; see especially *Abinger Harvest*, p. 269, and *Two Cheers*, p. 305.
[2] The allusion is to Keats.

novel's plot draws the principal characters toward this realization.

No less conspicuous is Forster's reverence for the influence of traditional rural life—the life of the closely-knit family whose roots are in the soil. As I. A. Richards observes, Forster's writings are characterized by "a special preoccupation, almost an obsession, with the continuance of life, from parent to child, with the quality of life in the sense of blood or race, with the preservation of certain strains and the disappearance of others."[3] His idea of family tradition is bound to his view of the part that Battersea Rise played in the Thorntons' lives, and to reminiscences of his own boyhood home in Hertfordshire. Of the latter he has written, "I took it to my heart and hoped, as Marianne had of Battersea Rise, that I should live and die there." (*Marianne Thornton*, p. 301) Actually, both houses were razed to make room for suburban tracts. Two of Forster's minor works, "The Abinger Pageant" (1934) and *England's Pleasant Land* (1938), were written to oppose this kind of "improvement." The point of both plays is that country people ought to cherish their local traditions, that a stand must be taken against the levelling force of urbanization.

Much of this sentiment can be related to Forster's critical view of the Industrial Revolution,[4] but it also has a more positive basis in his temperament. What he says of Ibsen and Wordsworth seems equally true of himself: he is haunted by the romantic possibilities of scenery. (*Abinger Harvest*, p. 88) The landscapes in his novels have an almost pantheistic vitality, and they are usually enlisted on the side of self-realization for the central characters. To be attuned to the spirit of the countryside is not simply to resist the shallowness of London, but to be awake to the full life of the senses, without which there is no real awakening of the soul. In *The Longest Journey* and *Howards*

[3] I. A. Richards, "A Passage to Forster; Reflections on a Novelist," *The Forum*, LXXVIII (1927), 918.

[4] See especially *Two Cheers*, p. 273.

End particularly, the question of achieving a proper relationship to the rural landscape is inseparable from that of understanding one's own nature and of putting oneself in fruitful connection with the past and the future.

The presence in Forster of such obviously romantic opinions as these may lead us to ask where the center of his thought really lies. Many of his attitudes belong among those that William James characterized as "tough-minded": empiricist, pessimistic, irreligious, fatalistic, pluralistic, and skeptical.[5] A mind of this quality supposedly prefers "the rich thicket of reality"[6] to all unifying abstractions. In Forster's writing, however, there are a few affirmations that are virtually religious; we do not feel that any amount of contrary evidence could weaken them. The inconsistency is especially interesting in Forster's case because it is not merely temperamental, but points to contradictions within the intellectual climate of his formative years.

Virtually all of Forster's beliefs owe something to his years at Cambridge. His undergraduate life at King's College, from 1897 to 1901, was a period of self-discovery that was made more brilliant by the drabness of his previous life as a day boy at Tonbridge. This is apparent from *The Longest Journey*, which is obliquely autobiographical, but it also shines through the biography of Lowes Dickinson. Forster's account of Dickinson's introduction to Cambridge, for example, is revelatory:

"He had no idea what Cambridge meant—and I remember having the same lack of comprehension about the place myself, when my own turn came to go up there. It seems too good to be real. That the public school is not infinite and eternal, that there is something more compelling in life than team-work and more vital than cricket, that firmness, self-complacency and fatuity do not between them compose the whole armour of man, that lessons may have to do with leisure and grammar with literature—it is difficult for an inexperienced boy to grasp truths so revolutionary. . . ." (*Dickinson*, p. 26)

[5] See *Pragmatism*, p. 22.   [6] *ibid.*, p. 55.

The Cambridge that Forster knew in 1897 had much in common with Leslie Stephen's Cambridge of 1850, though sweeping reforms (most notably the abolition of religious tests) had been instituted in the meantime. Perhaps the most important of these similarities, strengthened by the University's preeminence in mathematics and science at the end of the century, was a general reluctance to commit oneself about what Stephen had called the unknowable. There were, to be sure, conspicuous exceptions in both eras, but there remained a general atmosphere of common sense and empiricism as opposed to Oxford's idealism and theology.[7] Both the Clapham Evangelicals and their agnostic descendants profited from a Cambridge tradition of liberal dissent that dated from the early years of the Reformation.

Forster's college, King's, has relevant traditions of its own. Founded exclusively for Etonians, it gradually improved its academic status by broadening its membership and admitting only students who were reading for Honours. By Forster's day it had become a haven for sensitive young men, many of them scholarship boys, who were unmoved by the popular ideals of success, sportsmanship, and horseplay. Its Fellows were, and still are, noted for their democratic and affectionate interest in the undergraduates. "In its exquisite enclosure," writes Forster, "a false idea can be gained of enclosures outside though not of the infinite verities." (*Dickinson*, p. 104) "The infinite verities" is hardly the phrase of a caustic iconoclast, and may suggest that Forster's romanticism was nurtured at King's. The world of King's is a placid and cloistered one where the religion of intense friendship and the pursuit of the Good and the Beautiful can flourish without much disturbance from outside.

Still another fruitful tradition was that of the Cambridge Conversazione Society (the Apostles), the famous discussion group founded in 1820. Its membership at various times included Tennyson and Hallam, F. D. Maurice, Richard Trench,

---

[7] See Stephen, *Some Early Impressions*, pp. 13-16, 33-35.

Monckton Milnes, Walter Raleigh, Henry Sidgwick, A. N. Whitehead, William Harcourt, James Clerk-Maxwell, and G. E. Moore, among others scarcely less famous. Forster, Lowes Dickinson, Roger Fry, Leonard Woolf, Lytton Strachey, and J. M. Keynes were all Apostles. From the first the Apostles were characterized by skepticism, liberalism, and moral earnestness, as well as by the equally Forsterian trait of self-effacement.[8] Sidgwick reported that the discussions were marked by candor, humorous sarcasm, mutual respect, skepticism, and a willingness to entertain views opposed to one's own.[9] Forster, in writing of Cambridge discussion societies on the whole, emphasizes the same qualities. With their allowance for whimsicality, their deference to "truth rather than victory," and their informal friendliness, the societies "represent the very antithesis of the rotarian spirit." (*Dickinson*, p. 66)

Cambridge philosophy in Forster's day also deserves mention for its relevance to the Forsterian view of friendship. When Forster writes that personal relations, though never perfect, can "hint at perfection" (*Ibid.*, p. 78), he is expressing a measure of agreement with an Apostle, J. E. McTaggart, whose philosophy was much in vogue at the turn of the century. McTaggart believed in "a possible communion between individuals, each from an understanding of the other's essential nature, a communion that could transcend individual actions and fix itself only on the personality. . . ."[10] Forster was not a student of McTaggart's writings, but, as it happens, he was on close terms with two of the men with whom McTaggart claimed to be in "communion": Lowes Dickinson and Nathaniel Wedd. Dickinson, too, had a semi-mystical view of friendship. Like Plato and Shelley, two of his

---

[8] Alan Willard Brown, *The Metaphysical Society; Victorian Minds in Crisis, 1869-1880* (New York, 1947), p. 2. See also Frances M. Brookfield, *The Cambridge "Apostles"* (New York, 1907).

[9] See A[rthur] S[idgwick] and E[leanor] M. S[idgwick], *Henry Sidgwick; A Memoir* (London, 1906), pp. 34f.

[10] G. Lowes Dickinson, *J. McT. E. McTaggart* (Cambridge, England, 1931), pp. 77f. The sentence is by Basil Williams, who contributed one chapter of this book.

idols, Dickinson believed that the experience of love between two individuals has something of the divine in it.[11] Whether or not McTaggart's other friend, Nathaniel Wedd, shared this view I do not know; but he certainly could have passed along some of McTaggart's ideas to Forster, for he taught Forster Classics at King's, and it was "to him more than to anyone," Forster says, "that I owe such awakening as has befallen me." (*Dickinson*, p. 73)[12]

Forster's similarities to Lowes Dickinson do not end with their faith in personal relations, nor even with their agreement in political philosophy. The two men were friends for thirty-five years, and though Wedd may have "awakened" Forster, Dickinson's range of sympathies is suggestively close to Forster's own. The conjunction of skepticism and romanticism in Forster is anticipated in Dickinson, who might be said to illustrate both sides of Forster's temperament in extreme form. With McTaggart, he was rigorously agnostic toward every established religion while aspiring, in Virginia Woolf's words, "to climb the heights of the metaphysical Parnassus."[13] His Shelleyan religion of humanity led him to seek in poetry what he no longer found in Christ, and to work devotedly for the founding of the League of Nations. Though Forster does not expect the world to be saved through either poetry or international law, he does admire these things; he has Dickinson's notion of goodness without Dickinson's faith that it can be put into practice on a broad scale.

Forster and Dickinson are also close in their attitudes toward ancient Greece. Both of them connect Greece with the idea of accommodating bodily passion, and both therefore look to Greece as a kind of antidote to Christian asceticism. Dickin-

[11] See Dickinson, *After Two Thousand Years; A Dialogue Between Plato and a Modern Young Man* (London, 1930), *passim*, and Forster, *Dickinson*, pp. 37-43.

[12] The third of McTaggart's three "communing" friends was Roger Fry, who was not residing in Cambridge when Forster was an undergraduate; he became associated with Bloomsbury in 1910. See J. K. Johnstone, *The Bloomsbury Group; A Study of E. M. Forster, Lytton Strachey, Virginia Woolf, and Their Circle* (New York, 1954), p. 15.

[13] Virginia Woolf, *Roger Fry; A Biography* (New York, 1940), p. 102.

son originally went to Plato (and to Plotinus and Buddhism and Hinduism) to satisfy his thirst for esoteric religion, but after about 1890 he also steeped himself in Plato's theories of education, politics, and ethics. (see *Dickinson*, pp. 42-45) Forster is not a Platonist—he is wary of any philosophy that smacks of other-worldliness—but he shares Dickinson's view of Plato's importance: "The Greeks," he says, "—and Plato particularly—understand our political and social confusion, but they are not part of it, and so they can help us." (*Ibid.*, p. 46) For both Dickinson and Forster the Greeks stand for a reasonable and civilized acceptance of man's full nature, a circumventing of the modern extremes of inhuman machine-worship and morbid salvationism.

It would seem, however, that Dickinson's importance to the Bloomsbury group apart from Forster was not decisive. He had formed, at least as early as 1901, a "Discussion Society" to which Forster, J. M. Keynes, and probably others among the future Bloomsbury writers belonged,[14] but his greatest service was to introduce them to McTaggart, Bertrand Russell, and G. E. Moore—especially Moore.[15] Dickinson's thinking was in the last analysis a bit too vague and wishful for Bloomsbury's taste. Nevertheless, he was held in high respect for his integrity and lack of bombast, and something of his spirit may have been passed along. Lytton Strachey, writing to J. M. Keynes, said of Sir Walter Raleigh that "he belongs to the age before the flood —the pre-Dickinsonian era which is really fatal."[16]

[14] See *Dickinson*, p. 102, and R. F. Harrod, *The Life of John Maynard Keynes* (London, 1951), p. 63. Harrod corrects Forster's dating of the Discussion Society from 1904.

[15] See Harrod, *Keynes*, p. 63, and Forster, *Dickinson*, pp. 115f.

[16] Quoted by Harrod, *Keynes*, p. 111. Strachey's opinion of McTaggart, expressed in a pithy quatrain, shows the new generation's hardening against vague theologizing:

> McTaggart's seen through God,
> And put him on the shelf;
> Isn't it rather odd
> He don't see through himself.

Quoted by Charles Richard Sanders, *Lytton Strachey; His Mind and Art* (New Haven, 1957), p. 32.

It is worthwhile to bear in mind the dates of Forster's years at Cambridge when we consider the provenance of his ideas. The nucleus of what was to become Bloomsbury was formed in the Midnight Society, another discussion group, at Trinity College in 1899. Strachey, Saxon Sydney-Turner, Leonard Woolf, Thoby Stephen, and Clive Bell all belonged to this circle.[17] Forster, however, had been at Cambridge for two years before these men arrived, and had already undergone his awakening at King's. Keynes noted that the future Bloomsbury writers "did not see much of Forster" at Cambridge; Forster was "already the elusive colt of a dark horse."[18] Nor, according to Vanessa Bell, was he more than an occasional visitor to the later sessions in Bloomsbury proper.[19] Clive Bell, writing in 1956, even professed to be unaware that Forster had ever "been branded with the fatal name" of Bloomsbury.[20] The point to be drawn from these recollections is that Forster's "Bloomsbury" characteristics probably owe a good deal to the general Cambridge atmosphere as it was breathed by the "intellectual aristocracy" at the turn of the century. If Forster was able to exchange ideas with his Bloomsbury friends it was because their heritage and training gave them a common ground on which to meet.

To define Forster's relationship to Bloomsbury we must of course decide what Bloomsbury is—a question that has too frequently been oversimplified. G. E. Moore's *Principia Ethica* (1903), as everyone recognizes, is the central document for an understanding of Bloomsbury values. Keynes thought of Moore's impact on the Midnight Society as "the beginning of a renaissance, the opening of a new heaven on a new earth,"[21] and

[17] See Clive Bell, *Old Friends; Personal Recollections* (London, 1956), pp. 129f. J. M. Keynes arrived at Trinity in 1902.
[18] John Maynard Keynes, *Two Memoirs*, p. 81.
[19] See Annan, *Leslie Stephen*, p. 123n.
[20] Bell, *Old Friends*, p. 131. Also noteworthy is the omission of any mention of Forster in Duncan Grant's reminiscences of Bloomsbury meetings at the Stephen house in Fitzroy Square. See Duncan Grant, "Virginia Woolf," *Horizon*, III (June 1941), 402-406.
[21] Keynes, *Two Memoirs*, p. 82.

Lytton Strachey is said to have welcomed Moore's ascendancy with the cry, "The age of reason has come!"[22] It appears, however, that the Bloomsbury writers by no means allowed Moore to demolish their previous values, but rather accepted those parts of his philosophy which they were already disposed to believe.

Principia Ethica contains three main points. The first and most important is that the predicate *good* represents a simple, indefinable attribute which cannot be identified with anything actually existent. To equate good with pleasure, for example, as Mill does, or with evolution, as Spencer does, is to commit "the naturalistic fallacy." Instead of finding the predicate *good* in the world, we evaluate the world by reference to our instinctive and a priori sense of good.[23] Secondly, Moore held that the "complex wholes" of consciousness involved in the pleasures of human affection and the contemplation of beautiful objects are by far the most valuable things we can know. Good states of consciousness are, in fact, "the rational ultimate end of human action and the sole criterion of social progress."[24] And thirdly, Moore stressed the great difficulty of deciding empirically whether a given action will have good effects, and concluded that we should follow either of two courses in practical ethics. In cases where there is no generally accepted precedent we should consult our private evaluation of the situation, but otherwise we "can . . . be confidently recommended *always* to conform to rules which are both generally useful and generally practised."[25]

[22] Forster, *Dickinson*, p. 110. See also Leonard Woolf, "The Influence and Thought of G. E. Moore; A Symposium of Reminiscence by Four of His Friends," *The Listener*, LXI, No. 1570 (April 30, 1959), 756.

[23] Though Moore himself was a Platonist in assuming the reality of ethical attributes, his successful insistence on their indefinability led philosophers away from the *fin-de-siècle* vogue of Platonism. The inevitable next step was Wittgenstein's assertion that ethical predicates are not only indefinable but linguistically devoid of meaning.

[24] George Edward Moore, *Principia Ethica* (Cambridge, England, 1903), p. 189.

[25] *ibid.*, p. 164.

Considering these arguments as part of a total chain of reasoning, we have to agree with Bertrand Russell's opinion that Moore's ethics were "considerably distorted" by his Cambridge admirers.[26] J. M. Keynes himself acknowledges this distortion: "There was one chapter in the *Principia* of which we took not the slightest notice."[27] This was the chapter called "Ethics in Relation to Conduct," which defends ethical conformity. "We accepted Moore's religion, so to speak, and discarded his morals. Indeed, in our opinion, one of the greatest advantages of his religion, was that it made morals unnecessary—meaning by 'religion' one's attitude towards oneself and the ultimate, and by 'morals' one's attitude towards the outside world and the intermediate."[28] Needless to say, this is not a legitimate extension of Moore's emphasis upon art and personal relations. When Keynes and his friends decided to pursue these goals exclusively, they were behaving in effect as though "the Good" were simply equatable with art or love. They were committing the naturalistic fallacy.[29]

In all other respects, however, Moore's impact on Bloomsbury was decisive. Nothing mattered, says Keynes, but passionate contemplation of a beloved person, beauty, or truth, "and one's prime objects in life were love, the creation and enjoyment of aesthetic experience and the pursuit of knowledge."[30] Moore's analysis of aesthetic enjoyment, by emphasizing acuteness of cognitive judgment and propriety of emotion as well as intrinsic worth in the contemplated object, provided a rationale for the Bloomsbury emphasis on taste. Cultivating one's taste, indeed, seems to have had somewhat the same moral urgency

[26] See "The Influence and Thought of G. E. Moore," *The Listener*, LXI, 756.

[27] *Two Memoirs*, p. 82.

[28] *ibid.*, p. 82.

[29] Moore even argues that, all else being equal, conventional ethical behavior is preferable to unconventional because of the good example it sets (see *Principia*, p. 163). Nothing could be farther from the Bloomsbury fear of banality.

[30] *Two Memoirs*, p. 83.

that cultivating one's sense of duty had had for Bloomsbury's Evangelical predecessors. We may also note that Moore broke the last link connecting the Bloomsbury undergraduates to Utilitarianism. Both Keynes and Bell give him credit for exposing the fallaciousness of the greatest-happiness principle.[31] He inspired them to give themselves unashamedly to self-cultivation without worrying about a hypothetical general utility. And, finally, Moore's peculiar kind of Socratism had an effect upon Bloomsbury manners. Although Moore himself was a man of simplicity and unworldliness, his minute concern for definitions and his habit of peremptory cross-examination were copied in a semifrivolous spirit and became part of the *mystique* of Bloomsbury argumentation.

If we now ask ourselves whether Forster's ideas are in harmony with Moore's, the results seem impressive. Moore's affording a chief position to aesthetic enjoyment and personal relations, his freedom from Utilitarian ethical standards, his lack of interest in a life of action, and his anti-asceticism are all descriptive of Forster. Is Forster, then, a disciple of Moore's? "It was only for us, those who were active in 1903," says Keynes, "that Moore completely ousted McTaggart, Dickinson, Russell."[32] And Forster writes that although Moore "did carry the younger men by storm," he himself is "a complete outsider" to the nature of the influence. (*Dickinson*, p. 110) He remembers "the attractive blue cloth of the binding" of *Principia Ethica,* but he misdates its publication by two years and shows no firsthand acquaintance with its contents. (See *ibid.,* p. 111)

This is not to say that Moore's influence did not finally reach Forster, however deviously. Although most of the attitudes shared by Moore and Forster can be found in the early Lowes Dickinson,[33] the differences in intellectual emphasis between

[31] See *Two Memoirs*, pp. 96f., and *Old Friends*, p. 133.
[32] *Two Memoirs*, pp. 81f.
[33] Moore's refutation of Utilitarian ethics was famous and decisive, but was by no means the first attempt. Dickinson's own criticisms in *The Meaning of Good* (Glasgow, 1901, pp. 63-74) belong with a tradition of

Dickinson and Forster reveal the success of Moore's assault on romanticism. Dickinson's love of humanity is diminished to Forster's qualified trust in individuals, and Dickinson's quest for metaphysical truth becomes Forster's urbane curiosity, well tempered with pyrrhonism. Forster's political detachment also suggests the new generation. The Victorian sense of life as a pilgrimage, which Dickinson still shared (See *Dickinson*, p. 119), projected the dream of a Utopia, a City of God on earth, where all progress would culminate; Dickinson's Fabianism and his internationalism were still directed by this dream, pale and improbable as it seemed in the twentieth century. The followers of Moore, in contrast, saw life not as a pilgrimage but as an adventure, a series of discrete experiences whose value lay in the immediate moment of perception or contemplation. The First World War, though it brought an abrupt end to whatever liberal dreams had survived the Gladstonian era, was not needed to turn Forster and his friends away from Utopian politics. The doctrine of seeking the Good and the Beautiful only in personal relations and art had already been codified for them in *Principia Ethica*—whether Forster read the book or not.

Yet if we content ourselves with pinning the tag "Bloomsbury" on Forster, without considering his many ties to the previous generation, we may oversimplify his art as well as his intellect. Though he professes to disdain "the trailing garments of Shelley," for instance, Shelley presides like a patron deity over *The Longest Journey*, and it is Shelley who underlies his theory of art-for-art's-sake.[34] Though he speaks with amusement of Dickinson's inability to grasp Roger Fry's formalism, Forster himself has exactly the same blind spot; Fry used to take him to galleries because "He found it an amusing change to be with someone who scarcely ever saw what the painter had painted." (*Two Cheers*, p. 131) Forster has, indeed, never allowed his

---

anti-Benthamism that originated, however reluctantly, with John Stuart Mill in the 1830's.

[34] See *Two Cheers*, p. 94.

modern taste for the concise phrase and the refined symbol to extinguish his old-fashioned interest in storytelling and romance. His novels are closer in spirit to Hardy and Meredith, the literary idols of the turn of the century, than they are to Virginia Woolf.

Nor is Forster wholly immune from the Platonism and the Utopianism that he and his generation are supposed to have outgrown. We should bear in mind that he is perpetuating the tradition of McTaggart and Dickinson, not Moore, when he says that personal relations can "hint at perfection"; Moore would have reduced such a statement to nonsense with one stroke. Would Lytton Strachey agree that the human individual is "a divine achievement," or that his temple is "the Holiness of the Heart's Affection"? Or that beyond our daily affairs "There is the Beloved Republic to dream about and to work for through our dreams; the better polity which once seemed to be approaching on greased wheels; the City of God"? (*ibid.*, p. 11) This is really the voice of Lowes Dickinson speaking through Forster, and it is by no means a unique instance.[35]

The persistence of such atavisms in Forster may prepare us for the intellectual world of his novels, which is sometimes as remote from us as his manner is familiar. Even his most "advanced" novel, A *Passage to India*, strikes a faintly archaic note; it re-investigates the standard Victorian questions about God as if they had never been pronounced meaningless by pragmatists and linguists. Forster's agnosticism and romanticism, those delicate blooms from an earlier age, have remained curiously hardy in our inclement century. Beneath them, apparently stronger than any subsequent force in Forster's life, lies the Cambridge of Dickinson and Moore, with its own vital contradictions between idealism and empiricism, collectivism and individualism, religiosity and common sense.

[35] See, e.g., *Abinger Harvest*, pp. 29f., 285.

Five

THE LONGEST JOURNEY

The Longest Journey (1907), which Forster has repeatedly called his favorite of the five novels and the one in which he was most deeply engaged, offers us a close view of the various and sometimes conflicting influences we have traced in previous chapters. The view is close because Forster, writing only a few years after his graduation from Cambridge, was involved in essentially the same position as that of his semi-autobiographical hero, Rickie Elliot—the position of having to reconcile the sequestered world of his college with the demands of ordinary existence. The problem, however, is not simply one of "adjustment," of compromising the donnish temperament with the mundane. Forster's question is whether the purposeful, individualistic pursuit of the Good and the Beautiful—the way of life embodied in Lowes Dickinson and justified in ethical terms by G. E. Moore—has a proper right to existence at all. Will the pages of Shelley and Plato remain legible in the glare of everyday?

This is not, of course, the philosophic heart of *The Longest Journey*, but simply a question of practical ethics that Rickie Elliot must resolve. Cambridge does not stand for one philosophy or another, but for an attitude of inquiry, of open-mindedness and zeal for truth, that is challenged by the "outside world" in the novel. But as a philosophical novel *The Longest Journey* undertakes to cope with still broader matters. What is a man's relationship to his own past and his future, and to his ancestors and his heirs? What, indeed, is his relation to the cosmos at large? Where should he place his faith? Is the world One or is it Many? That a novel of some three hundred pages should

offer replies to these questions is evidence enough that its author had not been out of school very long. Yet *The Longest
Journey* is surprisingly rewarding when read in philosophical
terms. The rather tame adventures of Rickie Elliot reflect a
complex and intelligible drama between opposed views of existence, and this drama can show us the immediate workings of
Forster's art and thought.

To say that a book reveals its author is not, of course, to call
it a successful work of art; it is hard to disagree with those who
have found *The Longest Journey* uneven and sometimes grossly
clumsy in execution.[1] This line of criticism, however, has tended
to place the blame on Forster's confused vision of life; the novel
is alleged to be messy because Forster's thoughts are messy. I
should say, rather, that Forster presents an extremely dense *clash*
of visions, manipulated with conscious intelligence and brought
to a carefully prepared resolution. The novel's confusion is
aesthetic rather than thematic. Forster has difficulty in maintaining his narrative distance from Rickie Elliot, who is required
to bear meaning both as a spokesman for Forster and as a victim of certain errors and weaknesses. Because Rickie's mind
provides the controlling point of view behind the narrative, we
have to rely on him for most of our knowledge of the other
characters. Yet one of Forster's crucial points is that Rickie's
mode of vision is a falsifying one. There is, consequently, an
uneasy marriage of representation and irony in what Forster
permits us to see through Rickie's eyes. Forster's method of com-
pensating for this is to blurt out, every now and then, an exact
confession of what he himself wants the story to mean. The
total result is a hodgepodge of concealment and revelation that
does not make for smooth reading.

Forster's "confessional" passages, nevertheless, prove very
handy for the critic. The most significant of these, Chapter

[1] See, e.g., Trilling, *E. M. Forster*, p. 67, and John Harvey, "Imagination and Moral Theme in E. M. Forster's *The Longest Journey*," *Essays
in Criticism*, VI (October 1956), 418-433.

XXVIII, can be taken as a philosophical gloss on the total action of the book. It is a chapter unique in all of Forster's work, not only for its brevity but because it makes no mention of the characters or their immediate problems. Here is the entire chapter:

"The soul has her own currency. She mints her spiritual coinage and stamps it with the image of some beloved face. With it she pays her debts, with it she reckons, saying, 'This man has worth, this man is worthless.' And in time she forgets its origin; it seems to her to be a thing unalterable, divine. But the soul can also have her bankruptcies.

"Perhaps she will be the richer in the end. In her agony she learns to reckon clearly. Fair as the coin may have been, it was not accurate; and though she knew it not, there were treasures that it could not buy. The face, however beloved, was mortal, and as liable as the soul herself to err. We do but shift responsibility by making a standard of the dead.

"There is, indeed, another coinage that bears on it not man's image but God's. It is incorruptible, and the soul may trust it safely; it will serve her beyond the stars. But it cannot give us friends, or the embrace of a lover, or the touch of children, for with our fellow-mortals it has no concern. It cannot even give the joys we call trivial—fine weather, the pleasures of meat and drink, bathing and the hot sand afterwards, running, dreamless sleep. Have we learnt the true discipline of a bankruptcy if we turn to such coinage as this? Will it really profit us so much if we save our souls and lose the whole world?"[2]

Forster's question here is whether we should place our trust in a this-worldly or an other-worldly hope, in the "spiritual coinage" of man's soul, or rather in the "incorruptible" coinage of God. Man's soul is liable to "bankruptcies," that is, it may

[2] *The Longest Journey* (Norfolk, Connecticut, n.d.), p. 260.

ascribe value wrongly and is bound to be thwarted eventually
by the mortality of the objects of its faith. On the other hand,
if we place our allegiance in God we may find ourselves deprived
of richness in our present experience. The metaphor of coinage
was perhaps suggested to Forster by the Biblical phrase, "For
where your treasure is, there will your heart be also." Forster,
however, would reverse the two terms: where your heart is, he
implies, there will your treasure be. And his own decision is still
more directly an inversion of Scripture: "Will it really profit us
so much if we save our souls and lose the whole world?" Although he makes a token gesture of deference to the belief in
personal immortality, Forster clearly believes that our present
world is the only one that ought to concern us. Though we seem
doomed to failure, there is a "true discipline of bankruptcy"
which may somehow make our souls "the richer in the end."

This argument bears upon all the principal characters of *The
Longest Journey*, but most conspicuously upon Rickie Elliot.
Rickie's entire career may be viewed as an effort to "reckon
clearly." He has temperamental leanings toward both the ascetic
and the humanistic positions, and he vacillates precariously between renouncing life and committing himself recklessly to it.
Neither attitude, according to Forster's gloss, will be ultimately
profitable: Rickie must avoid asceticism and yet beware of the
"bankruptcy" that follows from overestimating the worth and
permanence of the people he loves. The tripartite structure of
The Longest Journey emphasizes Rickie's problem of arriving at
a moderate and discerning humanism, for the names of the
book's three sections, "Cambridge," "Sawston," and "Wiltshire,"
are representative of rival outlooks that contend for his loyalty.
At Cambridge he gives himself to the detached life of the mind,
as epitomized in his friend Stewart Ansell. At Sawston he is
dominated by his wife and his brother-in-law, Agnes and Herbert
Pembroke, whose values are those of the public school they administer: teamwork, self-sacrifice, conformity to rules and duties.
And in Wiltshire Rickie learns a kind of natural piety from

his half-brother, Stephen Wonham, who is so obviously a symbol of bodily freedom that some readers have refused to consider him a literal character at all.[3]

Rickie's problem is to bring together the "Ansell" and "Stephen" sides of himself, that is, to connect the life of the mind with the life of the body. Both Ansell and Stephen are individualists and humanists: to be loyal to them is, for Rickie, equivalent to being loyal to his own better self. Sawston, which lies between Rickie and his spiritual goal like a Cave of Error or a House of Pride, offers him two spurious rewards for capitulating to "society": sexual love (from his wife Agnes) and a position of authority (as a schoolmaster). Rickie's discovery that these temptations have ruined his life might be called the "bankruptcy" whose true discipline he tries to learn. And though the effort is only partially successful for Rickie, it does make Stephen Wonham "the richer in the end," as we shall explain.

If we take the word *asceticism* to mean the suppression of human values for the sake of incorruptibility, we may say that antiasceticism is the dominant theme of *The Longest Journey*. The very phrase, "longest journey," which is taken from Shelley's *Epipsychidion*, bears this force in the novel. The relevant lines from Shelley are these:

> I never was attached to that great sect,
> Whose doctrine is, that each one should select
> Out of the crowd a mistress or a friend,
> And all the rest, though fair and wise, commend
> To cold oblivion, though it is in the code
> Of modern morals, and the beaten road
> Which those poor slaves with weary footsteps tread,
> Who travel to their home among the dead
> By the broad highway of the world, and so

[3] See, e.g., E. K. Brown, "The Revival of E. M. Forster," *Yale Review*, XXXIII (1944), 673.

With one chained friend, perhaps a jealous foe,
The dreariest and the longest journey go.

(II. 149-159)

Shelley's attitude here toward the "one chained friend" or the "jealous foe" is reflected in Forster's treatment of Agnes Pembroke, who marries Rickie and forces him to "commend to cold oblivion" both Stephen and Ansell (the "fair and wise," respectively). Rickie's decline from self-loyalty and his eventual resurgence are exactly parallel to his degree of subservience to Agnes, and Forster reminds us at several points that we should see this fact in Shelleyan terms. At Cambridge Rickie comes across the passage from *Epipsychidion* and marks it "very good" in the margin, but two years later, when he has become engaged to Agnes, he rereads the lines and finds them "a little inhuman." (p. 147) When married, he is confident that "never again must he feel lonely, or as one who stands out of the broad highway of the world and fears, like poor Shelley, to undertake the longest journey." (p. 192) And when he has finally escaped from Agnes he announces to Herbert Pembroke: "I never did belong to that great sect whose doctrine is that each one should select —at least, I'm not going to belong to it any longer." (p. 283) At this point he finds a new pleasure in reading the poems of Shelley, "a man," Forster adds clumsily, "less foolish than you supposed." (p. 298) Such heavy-handed allusions leave us in no doubt that a simple equation is intended between Rickie's freedom from Agnes and his faithfulness to what Forster (now misquoting Keats) designates as "the holiness of the heart's imagination." (p. 240)

It is significant that both Stephen and Ansell, despite their profound differences of temperament, are distrustful of Agnes and opposed to the "longest journey" in general. Stephen, whose moral creed is simply "here am I and there are you," has no desire to find a soulmate: "Love for one person was never to be the greatest thing he knew." (p. 276) He is convinced, as he puts it, that "all one's thoughts can't belong to any single person." (p. 307) Ansell's view is identical with Stephen's, though phrased more aphoristically: "Man wants to love mankind; woman wants to love one man." (p. 97)[4] Ansell is a prophet of the religion of which Stephen is the living embodiment: the religion of freedom from spiritual constraint. Though he looks up at the dome of the British Museum reading room "as other men look at the sky" (p. 207), what he finds there is substantially what Stephen finds in the countryside of Wiltshire. Ansell (following George Meredith) calls it "the Spirit of Life." "Myself I've found it in books," he explains. "Some people find it out of doors or in each other. Never mind. It's the same spirit, and I trust myself to know it anywhere, and to use it rightly." (p. 209) Ansell does recognize it at his first contact with Stephen, and he does use it rightly: he persuades Rickie to accept Stephen as his brother.

Stephen and Ansell have, to be sure, very different motives for their common attitude toward the longest journey. Stephen fully intends to marry and eventually he does; his only reservation is his belief that "you can't own people." (p. 307) Ansell's misgivings, however, seem attributable to a basically homosexual temperament. His intense disapproval of Rickie's engagement to Agnes stems from simple jealousy as much as from his awareness that Agnes will make a poor wife. For, as he acknowledges to himself late in the novel, his feeling for Rickie has been one of love (see p. 238). In this light an early scene between Rickie and Ansell takes on a special meaning. The two boys have been lying in a meadow outside Cambridge, and Rickie gets up to leave in order to keep an appointment with Agnes. Ansell seizes him by the ankle:

" 'Don't go,' he said idly. 'It's much better for you to talk to me.'

---

[4] Ansell may have borrowed the thought from Byron, *Don Juan*, I. 1545f., but he could also have learned it from Lowes Dickinson. See Forster, *Dickinson*, p. 41.

" 'Lemme go, Stewart.'

" 'It's amusing that you're so feeble. You—simply—can't—get —away. I wish I wanted to bully you.'

"Rickie laughed, and suddenly overbalanced into the grass. Ansell, with unusual playfulness, held him prisoner. They lay there for [a] few minutes, talking and ragging aimlessly." (p. 79)

The nature of this "unusual playfulness" is not out of keeping with Ansell's general disaffection with women (see, for example, pp. 94, 98), nor with his confessed inability to cope with the facts of sex and birth (see p. 210). It is noteworthy that Agnes, who is more than a little possessive toward Rickie, is intensely jealous of Ansell (see p. 202).

These suggestions, which are by no means conspicuous in the total pattern of the novel, nevertheless take on a considerable importance when we discover that Rickie, too, is unable to live happily with a woman. The early speculation by one of Rickie's Cambridge friends that he is "a little effeminate" (p. 95) and Ansell's admonition that he is "not a person who ought to marry at all" (p. 97) seem to be at least partially borne out by his total surrender of authority to Agnes. Rickie, who suffers from a hereditary defect of lameness, has never regarded himself as altogether fit to raise a family, and when his one daughter by Agnes is born lame and soon dies of pneumonia, he concludes that he should never again attempt to have a child. He is not, strictly speaking, a homosexual, but his physical handicap and his effeminacy are such that the more genuine strains of homosexuality in Ansel strike a responsive chord in him.[5]

Rickie's vaguely homosexual imagination, indeed, seems largely responsible for his original interest in Agnes. He is attracted

[5] In this connection one is reminded of Rickie's early exchange of letters with Ansell on the subject of Rickie's engagement. When Ansell warns his friend against "the eternal feminine," Rickie answers that "this letter of yours is the most wonderful thing that has ever happened to me yet— more wonderful (I don't exaggerate) than the moment when Agnes promised to marry me." He assures Ansell that Agnes will never come between them, and asks rhetorically: "Can't I love you both?" (p. 98)

to her not for her own sake but because he has idolized the athletic prowess of her dead fiancé, Gerald Dawes; a single glimpse of Gerald embracing Agnes becomes his introduction to the idea of sexual love and his permanent emblem for it (see pp. 51-53). It is not Agnes, but the image of Agnes and Gerald together, that enraptures Rickie. When Gerald dies in a football match, Rickie forces Agnes to "mind" her loss because he himself minds it, and he marries her on the perverse assumption that both he and she will remain loyal to Gerald's memory. Thus Rickie interprets his role as a husband altogether vicariously. Having attached a masochistic significance to the fact that Gerald bullied him as a boy (see pp. 49-50), he is more than half willing to be bullied by Agnes, who has shared Gerald's embrace.[6]

This complicated rationale behind Rickie's marriage exposes his most incurable habit of thought and his greatest weakness: an inherent tendency to view his experience symbolically rather than realistically. Gerald and Agnes do not appear to him as human beings but as figures in an emblem of sexual passion, and thus he is unable to perceive the threat that Agnes poses to his spiritual freedom. Ansell, who lives wholly in a world of books, and Stephen, who is wholly "natural," are equally qualified to see Agnes as she is, but Rickie is blinded by his effort to equate the world of books to the world of nature—to find fixed literary symbols in his everyday experience. This temptation is particularly strong in his dealings with Stephen, who is entangled in Rickie's sense of his own identity. Rickie's morbid temperament is governed by the idea of the suffering that his beloved mother endured at the hands of his father, a philanderer and a hereditary weakling who has bequeathed his lameness to Rickie. When

---

[6] A similar motive may be involved in Agnes' willingness to marry Rickie. She too is incapable of genuine passion apart from Gerald, but she has heard of Gerald's early treatment of Rickie, and "she had a thrill of joy when she thought of the weak boy in the clutches of the strong one." (p. 63) The same sadist-masochist relationship that held between Gerald and Rickie is resumed between Agnes and Rickie.

Rickie first learns that Stephen is his illegitimate brother, he assumes that he and Stephen share the same father, and he willingly defers to Agnes' opinion that Stephen is a self-seeking boor. All is changed, however, when Ansell explains that Stephen is the son of Rickie's mother, not his father. In this revelation Rickie sees an opportunity of fulfilling his ambition to have a brother and, more importantly, to "resurrect" his dead mother. He and Stephen have, he thinks, "got behind right and wrong, to a place where only one thing matters—that the Beloved should rise from the dead." (p. 283)

We know from the "coinage" chapter that this effort of Rickie's cannot bring him out of his spiritual bankruptcy: "We do but shift responsibility by making a standard of the dead." Nevertheless, Stephen does possess a legitimate symbolic value both for Rickie and in the total scheme of *The Longest Journey*. This value hinges upon the other half of Stephen's parentage. We learn toward the end of the novel that Mrs. Elliot's lover, a man designated only as Robert, was a civilized and imaginative farmer, a "natural man," yet a highly articulate spokesman for naturalness. "As he talked, the earth became a living being—or rather a being with a living skin—and manure no longer dirty stuff, but a symbol of regeneration. . . ." (p. 264) This implausible person is himself a symbol of man's secular vigor and potential decency. He rejects the Christian antithesis between sensual and spiritual, admitting only that love, whether illicit or not, is more valuable than the barren "duty" of renunciation: he too is among the characters who win Forster's approval by placing an individual notion of propriety above a social one. He and Mrs. Elliot run off to Stockholm to achieve their liberty, but, significantly, Robert drowns as the two of them "raced for the open sea." (p. 271) First, however, Stephen is conceived, a boy who is destined to have "a cloudless spirit—the spirit of the seventeen days in which he was created." (p. 276) The reader need not be reminded that the actual begetting of a child takes something less than seventeen days, yet Forster means just what he says: Stephen's spirit is an expression of the whole undertaking of the trip to Stockholm, that is, of the symbolic rupture with society. When Stephen persuades Rickie to desert Agnes he performs the identical service that his father did for Mrs. Elliot. He intrudes the wisdom of nature into a custom-ridden marriage, enabling one of the partners to experience both the perilousness and the desirability of following "the heart's imagination."

This brings us to the question of the ultimate philosophy projected by *The Longest Journey* as a whole. It is evident from the size and complexity of Forster's plot that he is not leading us to a simple "moral" about the wisdom of the heart. Nor could we say that Platonic or homosexual friendship is presented as an absolute ideal. The Robert-Mrs. Elliot episode contradicts this, and Rickie correctly ascribes the failure of his own marriage to his shortcomings of character (see p. 313). Nor can we entirely reconcile Ansell's disinterested pursuit of truth with Stephen's anti-intellectualism. Stephen himself, though a model of independence and masculinity, is by no means a perfect character; through most of the novel he is something of a drunkard and a sullen bully. If we are to find a unifying principle in *The Longest Journey* I think we must look beyond the immediate moral issues to a larger question that is posed by the common situation of the various characters. Forster's attitude toward this question sets the tone of the novel and establishes the most important connection between the characters' adventures and Forster's own passages of commentary.

The central difficulty, as the "coinage" chapter suggests, is that of properly evaluating human life. How large is man when viewed against the backdrop of his universe? Is it possible, or even worthwhile, to uphold our private standards of value in a world that is indifferent to our existence? The issue is raised obliquely on the opening page of the book, in the form of still another question: what is real? The rather inept debate in Rickie's Cambridge room over the existence or nonexistence of an unperceived cow is, as Lionel Trilling observes, a clue to the novel's theme.[7] One of Rickie's friends, apparently under the momentary sway of Bishop Berkeley, argues that the cow ceases to exist when the perceiver removes his attention. Significantly, it is Ansell who takes the opposite stand: "Whether I'm in Cambridge or Iceland or dead, the cow will be there." (p. 11) Though he later denies the existence of Agnes, he does so on grounds that are at least superficially consonant with his original position. Seeing the gap between Agnes' true character and the Agnes whom Rickie thinks he knows, Ansell calls her "the subjective product of a diseased imagination." (p. 27) His point here is ethical rather than metaphysical, and elsewhere he is consistent in his anti-Berkeleyanism. Since he believes that there is a more or less unchanging world which exists independently of any human mind, and that no single person is equipped to perceive more than an infinitesimal fraction of this whole, he will not allow himself to be persuaded that his own experience is any less valid than another's. Unlike Rickie, he does not brood over the seeming isolation of Cambridge from the "great world," and at one point he states his philosophy outright:

"There is no great world at all, only a little earth, for ever isolated from the rest of the little solar system. The earth is full of tiny societies, and Cambridge is one of them. All the societies are narrow, but some are good and some are bad. . . . The good societies say, 'I tell you to do this because I am Cambridge.' The bad ones say, 'I tell you to do that because I am the great world'. . . . They lie. And fools like you [Rickie] listen to them, and believe that they are a thing which does not exist and never has existed, and confuse 'great,' which has no meaning whatever, with 'good,' which means salvation." (p. 77)

Ansell's sense of value hinges upon what we might call his cosmology; he feels that since the universe has no distinctive

[7] E. M. *Forster*, p. 67.

character after which we can model our lives, we must develop a private idea of "the Good" and cling to it at all cost. It is not coincidental that Rickie, who expects his Cambridge ideals to be refuted by the "great world," falls an easy victim to the Pembrokes' philosophy that "school is the world in miniature," nor that it is the unsymbolical, frankly bookish Ansell who rescues him from error. Ansell's notion of the Good is unclouded because he feels no need to seek confirmation for it in the outside world.[8]

One's notion of the Good need not be derived solely from books, however; Ansell himself confesses, as we have seen, that "some people find it out of doors." Robert and his son Stephen exemplify this possibility. This is not to say that they find nature itself an unmixed good or an Emersonian preceptor of moral truths, but simply that they find good *within* nature. Both Robert and Stephen are in agreement with Ansell over the necessity of maintaining a human code of values in opposition to the blind wastefulness of nature, but at the same time their own virtues—masculinity, practicality, independence of thought—seem somehow to have been drawn from the soil. They are strong because their sense of the Good is contiguous with their sense of reality in the countryside.

Rickie, by contrast, is burdened with two incompatible views of nature, one overly poetic and the other quite disillusioned and prosaic. His sense of beauty leads him to believe that "poetry, not prose, lies at the core" of the natural world (p. 201), but his Christian training and his own deformity, in conjunction with the "natural" cruelty that he witnesses among the pupils at Herbert Pembroke's school, convince him that nature is essentially wanton. He secretly understands that "Nature has no use for us: she has cut her stuff differently." (p. 78) In the suf-

[8] We may note in passing that Ansell's argument corresponds roughly to the main point in G. E. Moore's *Principia Ethica*. Ansell, like Moore, remains Platonistic in believing that ethical attributes really exist, but he also shares Moore's rejection of the "naturalistic fallacy" of finding these a priori attributes within the perceived "great world."

fering of a schoolboy he "perceived more clearly the cruelty of Nature, to whom our refinement and piety are but as bubbles, hurrying downwards on the turbid waters. They break, and the stream continues." (p. 221) And Stephen, too, presents Rickie temporarily with an instance of nature's fickleness. It seems the height of injustice that Stephen should be likely to perpetuate the worthless line of Rickie's father while Rickie himself is to die without an heir. Rickie shields himself from such reflections by seeking in his relationship with Agnes a purity altogether exempt from reality, and by composing a series of mythological fantasies about communion with nature—stories that are convincing neither to a publisher nor to Stephen, the touchstone of the "natural" in *The Longest Journey*.

Rickie's outlook is significantly altered, however, when he learns that Stephen is his mother's son, for this suggests to him that "natural selection" may preserve the best as well as the worst hereditary strains. To Rickie's emblematic imagination the crucial fact about Stephen is that he represents a survival of their wholly "spiritual" mother; his very existence strikes Rickie as evidence that the spiritual and the natural need not be contradictory. He comes to feel that we can perpetuate what we love only by accepting the earthly side of our lives as a legitimate fact—by living within nature rather than erecting a rival world of impossibly sexless ideals. This is the "clear reckoning" that emerges from his bankruptcy.

Stephen's own views on the natural world are far from irrelevant to Rickie's philosophical problem. Although he has no personal grievances against nature, he wonders "what lucky chance had heated him up, and sent him . . . into a passive world." "He was proud of his good circulation, and in the morning it seemed quite natural. But at night, why should there be this difference between him and the acres of land that cooled all round him until the sun returned?" (p. 274) His reaction to such doubts is in conspicuous contrast to Rickie's. Instead of clinging to a dualistic theology that gives a subordinate importance to the realm of nature, Stephen becomes an enthusiastic though inexpert freethinker: "He worried infinity as if it was a bone." (p. 106)

This phase is brief, but Stephen never abandons his contempt for religion, and Forster plainly intends us to see his attitude as at once more practical and more reasonable than a Christian one. The point is brought home in an incident that occurs while Rickie and Agnes are journeying to Cadover to visit Mrs. Failing, Rickie's aunt. Their train, as Stephen informs them, has struck and killed a small child. Mrs. Failing, the Christian, taunts Stephen with questions about the fate of the dead child's soul. Stephen's "natural" conscience is horrified by such an impersonal way of thinking about death. " 'There wants a bridge,' he exploded. 'A bridge instead of all this rotten talk and the level-crossing. . . . Then the child's soul, as you call it—well, nothing would have happened to the child at all.' " (pp. 112f.) Not believing, as Mrs. Failing does, that this present world is merely a way station to heaven or hell, Stephen places a high value on the preservation of life; he agrees with Forster that it will not profit us to save our souls and lose the world. And in this connection it is worth remembering that Stephen and Ansell share the same criterion for judging their acquaintances: "They must be convinced that our life is a state of some importance, and our earth not a place to beat time on." (p. 302)

The moral victory of humanism in *The Longest Journey* is costly but unmistakably plain. Rickie dies, unable to make use of his "clear reckoning," but in dying he saves Stephen from being crushed by a train—possibly the same train that killed the child. It is, perhaps, the train of indifference to human life, or, as James McConkey suggests, the train of temporality that threatens to sever the human past from the human future; it must be "bridged" by an intelligent reverence for life.[9] The bridge is built both in fact and in metaphor: Stephen survives

[9] See McConkey, *The Novels of E. M. Forster*, pp. 115-117.

to raise a family and to cherish the memory of Rickie and their common mother, and the final chapter of the novel projects a hope that Stephen and his children will hold their own against both "society" and mutability, the two enemies of humanistic value in *The Longest Journey*. The waste and decay that have befallen the other characters, however, make it fitting that even in the final scene of his happiness Stephen should be troubled by the ultimate metaphysical question of the novel: "He was alive and had created life. By whose authority? Though he could not phrase it, he believed that he guided the future of our race, and that, century after century, his thoughts and his passions would triumph in England. The dead who had evoked him, the unborn whom he would evoke—he governed the paths between them. By whose authority?" (p. 326)

The thematic weight of *The Longest Journey* is conveyed not only through the overt plot and Forster's passages of commentary, but more subtly through the manipulation of symbols. James McConkey is correct in arguing that the entire symbolic pattern of the novel is built around the characters' pursuit of uniformity and stability in a treacherously changeable world.[10] Just as the pervasive imagery of streams and rivers is employed to suggest the purposeless flux of nature and the difficulty of asserting our human sense of importance (as Rickie thinks, "We fly together, like straws in an eddy, to part in the open stream"; p. 78), so the imagery of chalk and chalk-pits shows us the other face of nature, its continuity and oneness. Ridges of chalk constitute "the fibres of England" (p. 147), uniting Cambridge and Wiltshire and implying a consistent "substratum" of natural impulse beneath the artificial distinctions of society. At one point, for example, Stephen twists Herbert Pembroke around and forces him to see the chalk of Salisbury Plain: "There's one

[10] See *ibid.*, pp. 107-117.

65

world, Pembroke," he insists, "and you can't tidy men out of it."
(pp. 323f.)

The humanistic theme of *The Longest Journey* depends upon
our simultaneous awareness of these contradictory symbols, of
what McConkey calls "the coexistence of unity with mutability."[11] As in *Howards End,* the central problem of the novel is
"Only connect": only connect the past with the future, the
mind with the body, the human with the natural. A sense of
difficulty and peril is essential to this undertaking, for the human
condition is itself perilous; we must recognize and acquiesce in
our tenuous position if we are to make use of the few opportunities for true meaning that are afforded us. This attitude is
summed up in the posthumous words of Rickie's uncle, Anthony
Failing, whose epigrams provide much of the moral gloss to *The
Longest Journey*: "Let us love one another. Let our children,
physical and spiritual, love one another. It is all that we can do.
Perhaps the earth will neglect our love. Perhaps she will confirm
it, and suffer some rallying-point, spire, mound, for the new
generations to cherish." (p. 311) *The Longest Journey* is full
of symbolic rallying-points, many of which fail to meet Forster's
austere standard of validity. The Catholic Church at Cambridge,
for example, "[which asserts], however wildly, that here is eternity, stability, and bubbles unbreakable upon a windless sea"
(p. 71), is clearly disparaged, for this description comes shortly
after Rickie has learned "once for all that we are all of us bubbles
on an extremely rough sea." (p. 70) Sawston School is an inadequate symbol for the opposite reason: by selling out to "society"
it has failed to assign any importance to private human values.
It is in Wiltshire, where man's life is properly related to the
earth, that the most convincing monuments stand: Salisbury
Cathedral and the burial mound of the Cadbury Rings (the
"spire" and "mound" respectively in Anthony Failing's credo).
Both are valid symbols because they assert the persistence of

[11] *ibid.,* p. 117.

human love amidst the forgetfulness of nature rather than apart from it.[12]

This criterion applies, of course, not only to the literal monuments in the novel but also to the memories and relationships that Rickie attempts to "immortalize," such as the voice of his mother, his brotherhood with Stephen, and the embrace of Gerald and Agnes—all of which he distorts by removing them from their natural context. Furthermore, Rickie's shortcomings as a writer appear to stem from this very inability to distinguish between symbol and prosaic fact. Most of his extravagantly allegorical short stories about communion with nature are products of his "Agnes" period, when "the heart of all things was hidden" from him. (p. 167) The difficulty with his stories is identical with the difficulty in his life: he permits his imagination to isolate a few moments of heightened experience and to forget the chaotic flux from which those moments were abstracted. After he has deserted Agnes and absorbed some of Stephen's matter-of-factness, he finds himself able to write a realistic novel which becomes posthumously successful.

So far I have said little of the autobiographical implications of *The Longest Journey*, but at this point the connection between Rickie's career and Forster's becomes too overt to be ignored. Rickie's allegory that literally puts Stephen to sleep is identical in plot with Forster's story, "Other Kingdom" (see

---

[12] It may seem inconsistent that Forster should praise a Christian cathedral in so un-Christian a novel, but this is not in real violation of his anti-asceticism. Salisbury has value because generations of simple villagers "have found in her the reasonable crisis of their lives." (p. 281) The ascetic side of Christianity is epitomized in Cadover Church, whose weak, cracked bell reminds Rickie of his own unsturdiness. Forster's contrast of this bell with the rich, harmonious bell of Salisbury emphasizes the difference between Rickie and Stephen. It possibly also recalls a passage from Nietzsche's *Genealogy of Morals*: "The right of the happy to existence, the right of bells with a full tone over the discordant cracked bells, is verily a thousand times greater: they alone are the *sureties* of the future, they alone are *bound* to man's future." (*The Philosophy of Nietzsche*. New York, 1927, p. 751.) The sentence could stand as an epigraph for the whole of *The Longest Journey*.

pp. 86, 140), and Rickie's other stories reflect the allegorical classicism of Forster's early fantasies. When Stephen drops the counterpart of "Other Kingdom" into a rain gutter we can hardly avoid concluding that a slur is intended upon Forster's own tales. And, in a broader sense, the thinness of Rickie's stories makes us ask whether *The Longest Journey* may not be, among other things, an implicit critique of the symbolic habit of mind and hence a statement of dissatisfaction with Forster's own overdependence on symbolism.

In one sense, to be sure, *The Longest Journey* merely perpetuates the chief use of symbolism throughout Forster's early fiction. Many of the short stories present their central characters with "symbolic moments" that must be seized and cherished.[13] Since "the years are bound either to liquefy a man or to stiffen him,"[14] it is the part of wisdom to transfix some moment of youthful endeavor and freedom in which one has been loyal to his finest instincts. The same idea appears prominently in each of the early novels. Caroline Abbott in *Where Angels Fear to Tread* (1905) is "saved" from Sawston values by an unforgettable glimpse of Gino Carella fondling his baby, and another character, Philip Herriton, is likewise saved by his memory of Caroline's passion for Gino. Though Philip's experience is hardly less vicarious than Rickie's, he has discovered "something indestructible—something which she, who had given it, could never take away."[15] And Lucy Honeychurch, the heroine of *A Room With a View* (1908), confronts her future husband in three such symbolic moments, each of which helps to free her from the hypocrisies of society.

This justification for symbolic thinking is spelled out by Rickie in *The Longest Journey*: "It seems to me that here and there in life we meet with a person or incident that is symbolical. It's nothing in itself, yet for the moment it stands for some eter-

---

[13] See *Collected Tales*, "The Road from Colonus," "The Story of a Panic," "Other Kingdom," "The Curate's Friend," "The Point of It," and "The Eternal Moment."

[14] "The Point of It," *ibid.*, p. 218.

[15] *Where Angels Fear to Tread* (New York, 1958), p. 183.

nal principle. We accept it, at whatever costs, and we have accepted life. But if we are frightened and reject it, the moment, so to speak, passes; the symbol is never offered again." (p. 158; see also p. 289) Rickie knows whereof he speaks, for he has had two such moments himself: his confrontation of Gerald and Agnes and his meeting with Stephen just after he has learned that Stephen is his brother. He has, in a sense, "accepted life" by remembering the Gerald-Agnes emblem of sexual passion. His subsequent tragedy, however, implies that this abstraction, this fixation, of Agnes has been destructive. And this is precisely the point at which *The Longest Journey* seems to mark a departure. It is no longer sufficient for the hero to experience a symbolic moment in order to be "saved"; he must also return to the prosaic everyday world and make his peace with "nature." The irony of Rickie's fate is that his newfound interest in nature (that is, in heterosexual love) is precisely what prevents him from *behaving* naturally; his unrealistic attitude toward Agnes draws him unawares into the heresies of Sawston. As for his second opportunity for symbolism, Agnes has, as she boasts (p. 159), prevented him from seizing it. Rickie's life from that day onward is a continual effort to recapture his true relationship to Stephen; but, since the crucial moment has come and gone already, the effort is doomed to failure. And in a parallel sense, Rickie's allegories are equally doomed by their unnaturalness. Because they imply that communion with nature is merely an ideal, an intellectual concept rather than a possible reality, they fail to support Rickie's meager faith that "poetry, not prose, lies at the core" of nature.

The significant connection between Rickie's art and Forster's would seem to be that both men are hampered by their latent skepticism about the availability of meaning. Forster is convinced, as Rickie is, that certain moments in life have a legitimate symbolic value, but he is also aware of the obverse of this: most moments are part of a senseless flux. While *The Longest Journey* upholds the value of true symbolism, most of its emphasis is laid on the negative side. The artist's virtually im-

possible task is seen to be that of the humanist as Forster out-
lined it in his "coinage" chapter: to seek for meaning only in
the real world, yet somehow to forestall the "bankruptcy" of
disillusionment. We see in Rickie's case that the only easy
course, the retreat to allegorical fancy, is both an artistic and
a moral error, and we infer from this that Forster is pressing
himself toward a more realistic ideal. As a novel of ideas, we
may say, *The Longest Journey* is an attempt to dramatize the
aesthetic consequence of Forster's pessimism.

This attempt is, to be sure, only partially successful. In foregoing the comic framework of *Where Angels Fear to Tread*
and *A Room With a View*, Forster occasionally lapses into
passages of sentimental Meredithian philosophizing, of which
the "coinage" chapter is perhaps the most extreme example.
The inconvenience is not permanent, however; in *Howards End*
Forster regains his urbanity of tone while managing to treat
the same serious theme he broached in *The Longest Journey.*
The "goblins" of panic and emptiness that are met and temporarily exorcised in that novel are representative of the same
misgivings that haunt Rickie Elliot, and they seem more conspicuous and menacing than in the earlier novel. And in *A Passage to India*, Forster's major achievement as a novelist, his
skepticism has in a sense become the subject of the book. No
effort is made to contradict the fear that certain knowledge
of God is unavailable; that our friendships, though important
to us, have no bearing on the rest of the universe; and that we
are doomed by our nature to be victimized by prejudice and
delusion. From insisting thinly that we ought to love one another, Forster passes to admitting that whether we do or not,
the gods will not take note of it. Rickie Elliot's bankruptcy,
which is presented as a result of personal limitations of character
and vision, is generalized in *A Passage to India* to encompass
the bankruptcy of any and every attempt to find human meaning endorsed by the physical universe.

Six

THE ITALIAN NOVELS

Although *Where Angels Fear to Tread* (1905) and *A Room With a View* (1908) straddle *The Longest Journey* in date of publication, they would seem to stand together in more important ways. The two "Italian" novels, both of which were undertaken before *The Longest Journey* was published, are similar in tone, in theme, and in setting. Most obviously, they are connected by their common use of Italy as a scene of action and a symbolic force. In these novels Forster partakes of the Romantic tradition of embracing Italy as the home of brilliance and passion, of emergence from the English fog of snobbery and moralism. Like Shelley and Browning, Forster finds Italy rich in moral and emotional extremes that make the stuff of melodrama; *Where Angels Fear to Tread* treats of violence as inevitably as *The Cenci* or *The Ring and the Book*. Forster's dominant mode, however, is not melodrama but social comedy, and Italy provides an inexhaustible fund of occasions for satire and surprise. The contrast in *The Longest Journey* between the spirits of Sawston and Wiltshire is resumed in the Italian novels, but it is much enlivened by Wiltshire's being replaced by Italy, where the Sawston virtues are ineffective and unknown. The English visitors, many of whom harbor a lurking romanticism beneath their *sang-froid*,[1] find themselves in a world that is both alien

---

[1] Cf. Forster's "Notes on the English Character": the inhibited English "go forth into a world that is not entirely composed of public-school men or even of Anglo-Saxons, but of men who are as various as the sands of the sea; into a world of whose richness and subtlety they have no conception. They go forth into it with well-developed bodies, fairly developed minds, and undeveloped hearts. And it is this undeveloped heart that is largely responsible for the difficulties of Englishmen abroad. An undeveloped heart—not a cold one." (*Abinger Harvest*, p. 5)

and seductive, and the wide range of their responses—from puritanical recoil to complete surrender—generates the main action of both novels.

The moral issue in the Italian novels is the familiar one of whether we should heed the voice of passion or that of respectability. Forster believes in passion and eventually forces his characters to bow to it, but he is also aware of its dangers; we are not asked simply to agree that the Italian heart is preferable to the English spine. Still, the moral world of these novels is a relatively simple and schematic one. In *The Longest Journey* a Hardy-like sense of tragedy broods over the entire novel; however Rickie Elliot decides to behave, his fate is apparently controlled by complicated external forces. Here, however, Forster sees to it that his characters are rewarded or punished according to whether they adopt the right attitude toward passion. The universe of these novels, in other words, is comic rather than realistic. And this indicates what seems to me the most important difference between the Italian novels and the other three— namely, that here Forster's problematic metaphysics are not dialectically worked out within the plot. The "view" that Lucy Honeychurch must accept in *A Room With a View* is certainly a view of man's place in the universe, but her acceptance of it is merely symbolic; she is really concerned only with fulfillment in love. In neither of the Italian novels does Forster use his plot to extend or resolve his doubts about the underlying meaning of life.

Where Angels Fear to Tread and *A Room With a View* are thus self-contained and highly polished books. Instead of the internal strain that one feels throughout *The Longest Journey*, with its concentration on the soul of a single character and its groping for an adequate philosophy of man, we have novels that never threaten to crack the mold of their plots. Their meaning is largely ethical, and Forster is quite certain about his ethics. His certainty manifests itself in the form of ironic control over narrative language and the total structure of plot.

With the metaphysical background virtually eliminated, the social foreground can be rendered with an easy assurance of tone and a deft manipulation of comic adventure. Since the theme is now simple and clear, the reader's interest is drawn not to subtlety of meaning but to verbal and dramatic irony. Each of the Italian novels is tightly stitched together by this irony and by what Forster calls "rhythm"—the use of repetition and variation to strike recurrent chords in the reader's mind.[2] Forster himself as a moral commentator is somewhat less conspicuous than he is in *The Longest Journey*. We are expected to see through the "wrong" characters without his help, and to turn our attention to the suspense of his well-made plots.

The continuity of ethical concern between *Where Angels Fear to Tread* and *The Longest Journey* is neatly suggested in the fact that Sawston appears under the same name in both novels.[3] The opposing outlook is now represented by Monteriano, an Italian village quite isolated from the middle-class proprieties that the Sawstonians will import to it. The road to Monteriano "must traverse innumerable flowers." (*Where Angels Fear to Tread*, p. 25) Birth, love, and death compose the visible fabric of existence there, and the human tendencies that are most efficiently thwarted in Sawston are openly expressed: extravagance, superstition, theatricality, violence, coarse democracy among men, and ruthless subjugation of women. These are not "virtues" for Forster, but they help to complete the limited picture of reality available at Sawston. To acknowledge their right to existence is to loosen the grip of Sawston's provinciality, and hence, in Forster's private ethics, to be "saved." This is what Philip Herriton and Caroline Abbott, the principal English characters, manage to do (see *ibid.*, p. 112). It is inevitable that the character who remains least vulnerable to Monteriano's ap-

[2] See *Aspects of the Novel*, pp. 235-242.

[3] We might also note that "a certain Miss Herriton" is mentioned in *The Longest Journey* (p. 174) as a suitable matron for the boardinghouse of Herbert Pembroke's school. This is probably the Harriet Herriton of *Where Angels Fear to Tread*.

73

peal turns out to be the villainess of the novel. Because she cannot accommodate or understand passion, Harriet Herriton misjudges Gino Carella, the incarnation of Monteriano's spirit. Gino is at once brutal and tender, a bad husband but a good father, venal in some matters but incorruptible in others; one must be morally flexible to see his nature in its true colors. Harriet's puritanical loathing of Gino prompts her to "rescue" his baby from him by kidnapping it, and the result of her meddling is fatal.

Reduced to schematic terms, the plot of *Where Angels Fear to Tread* consists of the gradual exposure of four Sawstonians to Monteriano. In each case it is Gino Carella who exercises the decisive influence. Lilia Herriton, who is a Sawstonian only by marriage and widowhood, succumbs at once to Gino's raw masculinity; Gino appears to her as the embodiment of a freedom the Herritons have kept from her ever since she married their son. Lilia's view of Gino, however, is as wrong in its way as Harriet's. Her vulgarity of judgment prevents her from seeing, until it is too late, the immense social gulf between Gino and herself. After their marriage Gino treats her as a slave; he exhibits flashes of sadism which terrify her; and he betrays the marriage bed without a flicker of remorse. Lilia's death in childbirth, and the later death of her baby during Harriet's kidnapping, are palpable symbols of the danger of thinking that the two opposite cultures can be easily reconciled. In retrospect we see that the only possibility of success for the Gino-Lilia marriage would have been a mutual interest in sex. In fact, however, the passion of the supposedly cold Northerner, Lilia, has not been shared by the supposedly amorous Latin, Gino. Gino's "first great desire, the first great passion of his life" (p. 67) is his wish for a son, an heir to perpetuate his own existence beyond the grave. Neither Lilia nor Harriet can take account of this passion, for it does not belong in either of their hackneyed outlines of the Italian character.

Caroline Abbott, Lilia's chaperone in Italy, is both more in-

telligent and more inhibited than Lilia; at the beginning of
the novel, at least, she is an orthodox representative of Sawston's belief in decorum. But Monteriano and Gino in particular eventually succeed in evoking a Caroline who was quite
unknown in Sawston. Even at the outset she fails in her mission
to save Lilia from being seduced by Italy, for she secretly shares
Lilia's desire for freedom. As the novel progresses Caroline is
both increasingly reminded of her commitment to Sawston
morality and increasingly attracted to Gino as a man. The crucial moment in her internal debate is her realization, in watch-
ing Gino bathing his child, that he is the very image of an ideal
father. "The horrible truth, that wicked people are capable of
love, stood naked before her, and her moral being was abashed."
(p. 136) Caroline herself falls in love with Gino, not in the gen-
teel way that might be condoned in Sawston but "because he's
handsome, that's been enough." (p. 181)

Caroline's whole previous frame of judgment is thus shattered; she is forced by the blossoming of her own nature to reject Sawston's pious convictions as to what is acceptable or
objectionable. This is not to say, however, that she becomes
free to live as she pleases. At best, she learns exactly what it is
that she has excluded from her life; her return to Sawston at
the end is a frank admission of the impossibility of fulfillment.
In a tragic sense, though, her character has been enlarged and
ennobled by what she has experienced. In the eyes of Philip
Herriton "she seemed to be transfigured, and to have indeed
no part with refinement or unrefinement any longer." (p. 183)

The third visitor to Monteriano, and the one whose mind
we are allowed to examine most closely, is Philip Herriton. His
provinciality is more complicated than that of most Sawstonians, for he has already travelled in Italy and pronounced it in-
finitely superior to home. His sister Harriet is scandalized by his
seemingly cosmopolitan disdain for the sacred institutions of
Sawston: "The Book Club, the Debating Society, the Progressive Whist, the bazaars." (pp. 13f.) It is Philip, in fact, who

urges Lilia to visit Monteriano and to love and understand the Italian people—a piece of advice he soon regrets when he learns how literally and fully it has been accepted. He and Harriet together rush off to Monteriano to prevent the wedding with Gino (which has already taken place). Philip, however, is still an Italophile at heart. Like Caroline, but in a more bookish way, he secretly approves of Lilia's marrying into the land of pageantry and passion, and he mentally stipulates that he will not oppose the match if it is really "acceptable." Gino, however, is not a Renaissance prince but the unemployed son of a dentist, and when Philip hears this his Baedeker vision of Italy is suddenly closed off:

"Philip gave a cry of personal disgust and pain. He shuddered all over, and edged away from his companion. A dentist! A dentist at Monteriano. A dentist in fairyland! False teeth and laughing gas and the tilting chair at a place which knew the Etruscan League, and the Pax Romana, and Alaric himself, and the Countess Matilda, and the Middle Ages, all fighting and holiness, and the Renaissance, all fighting and beauty! He thought of Lilia no longer. He was anxious for himself: he feared that Romance might die." (p. 26)

This is only the first of a series of reassessments of Italy in Philip's mind. At Monteriano he finds it increasingly hard to remain disillusioned, until one day he finds that he agrees entirely with Caroline's low opinion of Sawston. "There is no power on earth," he declares at this stage, "that can prevent your criticizing and despising mediocrity—nothing that can stop you retreating into splendour and beauty—into the thoughts and beliefs that make the real life—the real you." (p. 78) This dictum, which is the heart of Ansell's advice to Rickie Elliot throughout *The Longest Journey*, goes along with an acceptance of Monteriano as a romantic image of the buried life; Philip, like Rickie in his dell at Madingley, is fortifying himself to resist the spurious "great world" of Sawston. Again, however, like Rickie, he finds himself caught up in Sawston's hypocrisies, and after only seven months at home he has lost his sense of romance once more. (pp. 79-81) Now when he is charged to return to Monteriano to bribe Gino into giving up his baby, he goes as a loyal agent of his sister.

This time, however, Philip and Gino meet entirely on Gino's ground, in circumstances such that the vulgarity and irresistible charm of Monteriano are inseparable. Philip has been prepared to revise his low opinion of Gino by the simple fact of Caroline's having told him that Gino admires him; flattery leads him to conclude that "romance had come back to Italy; there were no cads in her; she was beautiful, courteous, lovable, as of old." (p. 111) Though there is little that is courteous or beautiful in the opera performance Philip witnesses that night, there is much that is lovable. His reaction to the noisy, ugly, but effusively human spectacle is the reverse of Harriet's, and when Gino spies him and insists that he desert Harriet's box to join him, Philip delightedly agrees. The episode is an hilarious symbolic tug-of-war between Sawston and Monteriano, and, equally, between natural self-expression and snobbish decorum. Monteriano's victory is unequivocal. From this point on Philip is sympathetic with Gino, and though he fails to oppose Harriet strongly and hence fails to prevent the disastrous kidnapping, he remains on Gino's side—even after Gino in his grief has attempted to murder him. The scene of this assault ends with a tableau of Caroline holding the bereaved Gino's head upon her breast. In taking note of the elemental compassion and dignity of her role, Philip becomes assured "that there was greatness in the world. . . . Quietly, without hysterical prayers or banging of drums, he underwent conversion. He was saved." (p. 173) Though his worship of Caroline is not reciprocated (any more than is Caroline's love for Gino) both he and Caroline have found in Monteriano a sense of life's possible majesty.

The fourth visitor is Harriet, who has, in Philip's description, "bolted all the cardinal virtues and couldn't digest them." (p. 13) She alone remains immune to Monteriano and hostile to

Gino, and Forster will not let us forget that it is her Low-Church fervor, her insensitivity to all distinctions save moral ones, that blinds her. She typifies what Caroline calls the "petty unselfishness" (p. 76) of Sawston; her basic flaw is simply to be "the same in Italy as in England." (p. 114) Inspired by the Old Testament[4] and looking "like some bony prophetess—Judith, or Deborah, or Jael" (p. 160), she steals Gino's baby. The baby literally suffocates in her hands. The overturning of her carriage is the overturning of narrow Sawston morality, and her subsequent nervous collapse is the collapse of Sawston complacency when confronted by too sudden and too brilliant an exposure to reality.

The scene of the crash, which is the dramatic catastrophe of the novel, is packed with "rhythmical" elements that draw together the main thematic strands. When Philip, who is technically innocent of the kidnapping, discovers that Harriet is holding Gino's swaddled baby, he recalls that he has last seen the baby "sprawling on the knees of Miss Abbott, shining and naked, with twenty miles of view behind him, and his father kneeling by his feet." (p. 160) The recollection provides a stark effect of *chiaroscuro*, for now Gino and Caroline have been replaced by Harriet, the stiff and spinsterish enemy of life; there is no "view" in either sense of the word; the baby is not naked but heavily wrapped, not bronze but nearly invisible in the wet darkness. Furthermore, it is crying inaudibly, not yelling as in the other scene; we are reminded of Gino's assurance to Caroline, "If he cries silently then you may be frightened." (p. 138) Even the olive groves outside Monteriano, which have previously been described as "terrible and mysterious" (p. 56), contribute to the air of disaster here. They are only partly visible in the autumnal rain as the death carriage reels past them, but they are felt as a kind of insidious force of retribution. Italy is about to

---

[4] Harriet leaves for the kidnapping with her Bible open to Psalm 144:1: "Blessed be the Lord my God who teacheth my hands to war and my fingers to fight." (*ibid.*, p. 157)

show its displeasure with those who have been insensitive to its full-bodied life. Violets have previously been identified with passion, and the baby dies in "that little wood where violets were so plentiful in spring." (p. 162)

Rhythmical elements of this sort can be found on virtually every page of *Where Angels Fear to Tread*, though rarely with this degree of concentration. Wherever Forster's "rhythms" become really conspicuous, they verge on symbolism. Such, for example, is his mention of one of Monteriano's medieval towers, which is said by Philip to reach up to heaven and down to hell. Philip adds, all too pointedly, "Is it to be a symbol of the town?" (p. 113) Later, just when Harriet is snatching the baby, Philip gazes vacantly at this tower: "He could only see the base, fresh papered with the advertisements of quacks." (p. 157) The reminiscence here is subtle; not only do we recall the previous reference to "heaven and hell," but we are also meant to see an identity between petty quackery and Harriet's Christian zeal.

The "internal stitching" of *Where Angels Fear to Tread* extends from the very dimmest threads—such as Gino's identical stance before menacing his wife and before really attacking Philip (see pp. 58, 168)—to obvious "literary" themes, such as the occasional references to the "New Life" (Dante's *La Vita Nuova*) that Italy affords. Occasionally, too, a seemingly offhand quotation will have a serious thematic relevance. One of Gino's first actions in the novel is to recite the opening lines of the *Inferno* (p. 32), and we later remember that each of the principal characters is more or less "in the middle of the journey of our life"; that two of them, Philip and Harriet, "come to themselves in a dark wood" (where the baby is killed); and that "the straight way is lost" to every character until the drama has been acted through. Such allusive subtlety, I repeat, can only succeed in a work whose themes and authorial point of view are under perfect control from the beginning.

Lionel Trilling is right in comparing *Where Angels Fear to Tread* to *The Ambassadors*, both novels being concerned with "the effect of a foreign country and a strange culture upon insular ideas and provincial personalities."[5] The comparison can be worked out in considerable detail—so far, indeed, that a direct influence of James's novel on Forster's seems possible. Philip Herriton's education is close to Lambert Strether's in many ways. Both men come from a small town that is ridden by a Calvinistic fear of sex, and both turn against this quality in the course of a half-hearted mission to rescue a fellow-countryman from seduction by a European. Both, too, fall short of fully remodelling their lives according to their new, more liberal picture of human possibility—though both of them briefly entertain this ambition in the form of contemplating marriage to a woman who shares their point of view. They return whence they came, resigned to living in surroundings which they no longer consider sufficiently various or vital. Furthermore, Strether's incessant shifting of his attitude toward Paris is matched by Philip's toward Monteriano; they alternately overestimate and underestimate the foreign culture until at last they can accept its crude and beautiful elements together.

Thus the most important similarity of all is that Strether and Philip reach an understanding of what Forster designates in *The Longest Journey* as good-and-evil—the enormous moral complexity of the world. The concern for rectitude that is exaggerated in Sawston and Woollett cannot be altogether discarded, nor can the secularity of Monteriano and Paris; both must be retained if one is to be faithful to the truth of things. Yet Strether and Philip, being passive intellectuals by nature, are aware that life *cannot* be seen steadily and whole. They are paralyzed by the very magnitude of what they have learned, and their return to Woollett and to Sawston is an admission that the whole life of man cannot be mirrored in a single limited

[5] Trilling, *E. M. Forster*, p. 52.

existence. As Philip sees it: "Life was greater than he had supposed, but it was even less complete. He had seen the need for strenuous work and for righteousness. And now he saw what a very little way those things would go." (p. 177)

If *A Room With a View* (1908) is more frankly comic in plot than *Where Angels Fear to Tread*, it is quite equivalent in theme; in fact, the later-published novel is the more obviously connected to Forster's serious philosophy. George Emerson, the hero, has a "view" in the sense that he is concerned over man's apparent tininess and isolation in the universe; he is obsessed by the sort of awareness that Philip Herriton seems on the brink of acquiring at the very end of *Where Angels Fear to Tread*, and which Rickie, Ansell, and Stephen all have in *The Longest Journey*. Cecil Vyse, the unsuccessful suitor who is the butt of much of Forster's humor in the present novel, has no view at all; and Lucy Honeychurch, the heroine, ratifies George's view when she decides to marry him instead of Cecil. In this innocuous sense *A Room With a View* is a philosophical novel; and, indeed, this level of reference gives an unorthodox twist to the traditional comedy of manners. In most works of this genre the humor derives from the failure of certain characters to fulfill their social roles, whereas here the comic characters are precisely those who take society too seriously. The only ones who survive Forster's satiric barbs are those whose "view" enables them to see through the social code and recognize their enduring relationships to nature and their fellow men.

These relationships are defined for us quite dogmatically by George Emerson's father, whose role is comparable to Anthony Failing's in *The Longest Journey*. Mr. Emerson, as we might expect, prefers the unconscious life of instinct to the repressions of society. His humanism, like Mr. Failing's, is sharpened by a romantic sense of doom. He and George agree "that we come

81

from the winds, and that we shall return to them; that all life is perhaps a knot, a tangle, a blemish in the eternal smoothness."[6] Although this reflection fills George with adolescent *Weltschmerz*, it makes his father only more determined to assert the Spirit of Life. George's despair represents the state of mind of, say, Mill and Carlyle in their period of disillusionment with human hopes, while the ebullient Mr. Emerson represents the stage of recovery and new-found faith in humanity. His language on this subject is actually borrowed from *Sartor Resartus*: he asks Lucy to help George realize "that by the side of the Everlasting Why there is a Yes—a transitory Yes if you like, but a Yes." (p. 49)

Our awareness of the Everlasting Why in *A Room With a View* makes "society" appear not merely undesirable but positively sinister; by providing an illusion of completeness to lives, such as Lucy Honeychurch's, that are actually very constricted, society obscures the pressing need for sincerity and fidelity to instinct. The novel's happy conclusion, while anticipated as the proper ending to a comedy, is also a last-minute rescue from real disaster. In accepting George Emerson, Lucy effectively resigns from "the vast armies of the benighted, who follow neither the heart nor the brain, and march to their destiny by catchwords." (pp. 265f.)

It may be objected that this way of treating a rather frothy social comedy is disproportionately solemn. I agree. The disproportion, however, already exists within *A Room With a View*. While Forster wisely refrains from adopting too much of the Emersons' tone of profundity, their philosophy remains the thematic center of the book. Forster's sympathy with it is disguised, however flimsily, in his comic narrative manner. Unlike, say, D. H. Lawrence, he does not strike out directly at the social restraints that are keeping his heroine from self-fulfillment. Rather, he allows the code of the intolerant English tourists to

[6] *A Room With a View* (Norfolk, Conn., n.d.), p. 49.

provide an easy, though false, interpretation of the plot. We are not deceived by this technique for a moment, but we are grateful for having it; it keeps the novel on a keel of good-humored irony that is sometimes menaced by the weighty sincerity of the Emersons.

When we look at Forster's setting, characters, and plot without considering the Emersons' flights of agnostic religiosity, we find the elements of a thoroughly traditional love-comedy. The background of Florence, Fiesole, and rural England is appropriate for both romance and the exercise of snobbery. Lucy is a two-dimensional heroine; if we simply remember that she is a pretty girl who would like to be more passionate and honest than she is allowed to be, we have a key to everything she says and does in the novel. Stripped of his aphorisms—and, in one scene, of his clothes—George Emerson is an acceptably normal suitor, against whose attractive openness Cecil Vyse is seen as a stock example of the priggish rival. Nor is Lucy wanting in well-meaning friends and relations to help her undervalue the hero until the proper moment for reversal. The opposition of personalities is so bright that the plot, aided by a series of improbable comic coincidences, unfolds itself with a neat inevitability, in patent contradiction to the Emersons' opinion that "things don't fit." (p. 49)

This plot revolves around the familiar symbolic opposition between geographical influences, but less clearly so than in *Where Angels Fear to Tread*. The environs of Florence are sufficiently romantic and evocative of passion, but, on the other hand, so is the Surrey estate of the Honeychurches, and the "Gino" of this novel is George Emerson, an Englishman. It is also noteworthy that Lucy's upbringing has not been especially prudish or hypocritical. If we ask, then, what is the repressive force that opposes fulfillment for Lucy, the answer is not England but English Christianity—or, more precisely, watered-down English Puritanism.

Two Anglican priests, for example, play important roles in the general conspiracy to keep George and Lucy apart. The chaplain in Florence, Mr. Eager, is a pious fraud who succeeds in turning Lucy away from the Emersons early in the novel. George and his father have volunteered to trade their rooms in a Florentine pensione with Lucy and Charlotte Bartlett, her cousin and chaperone, so that the two ladies can have a view of the city, and this offer is accepted after Charlotte's exaggerated concern for propriety has been appeased. Lucy encounters George Emerson twice more by chance and finds him more interesting than she cares to admit; on the second occasion she half-willingly submits to a passionate kiss. By this time, however, the Reverend Eager has told Charlotte and Lucy what he knows about the Emersons. Not only are they Socialists, disbelievers, and the descendants of laborers, but Mr. Emerson is a criminal as well. He has "murdered his wife in the sight of God." (p. 90) The effect of this innuendo is to make the Emersons more appealing to Lucy; she cannot believe the accusation but it adds to the romantic air of Florence, "a magic city," she thinks, "where people thought and did the most extraordinary things." (p. 91) Lucy's instinctive fair-mindedness is also activated by this slur on the Emersons, and she unknowingly begins to take their part. The ultimate result of Mr. Eager's words is the reverse of what he intends: Lucy discovers that it was Mr. Eager himself, not Mr. Emerson, who was the "murderer"; he harried Mrs. Emerson to death by convincing her that her son George had contracted typhoid fever as a result of his not having been baptized.

The other priest, Mr. Beebe, takes an opposite role through most of the novel. At the beginning he mediates the exchange of rooms over Charlotte's protest, and he is the organizer of the picnic that ends in the sudden embrace. He is tolerant, sympathetic, and witty—so much so, remarks Lucy indiscreetly, that "no one would take him for a clergyman." (p. 23) Toward the end of the novel, however, we come to suspect that his humanism is only skin-deep. His reaction to the breaking of Lucy's and Cecil's engagement is revealing: "His belief in celibacy, so reticent, so carefully concealed beneath his tolerance and culture, now came to the surface and expanded like some delicate flower. 'They that marry do well, but they that refrain do better.' So ran his belief, and he never heard that an engagement was broken off but with a slight feeling of pleasure." (p. 284)[7] This secret reasoning would appear to be harmless, since the reader, too, is glad the engagement is over, but another circumstance casts a darker light on it. Mr. Beebe has just conferred with Charlotte over the necessity of Lucy's embarking at once for Greece, and Mr. Beebe, not knowing that Charlotte's motive is a desire to thwart George Emerson, has agreed to plead this cause with Mrs. Honeychurch. At the last minute Mr. Emerson meets Lucy in Mr. Beebe's rectory and forces her to see that she loves George and must marry him, but Mr. Beebe tries to prevent the meeting and nearly succeeds. This amiable and seemingly harmless man becomes dangerous in the crucial scene of the novel; and, of course, it is his Christian distrust of the body that lies behind his action.

The anti-Christian theme of A Room With a View applies to Charlotte and Cecil, too, but in their cases a lurking asceticism is indistinguishable from enslavement to social form. Charlotte's puritanical education has kept her from any notion of possible comradeship between the sexes, and she does her best to drive Lucy into a barren spinsterhood like her own. Some of her obstructive advice, such as her refusal at first to accept the Emersons' rooms, springs merely from a respect for decorum; but later, when she begins to see the seriousness of George's feeling for Lucy, she deliberately attempts to turn Lucy against him. It is she who interrupts the embrace on the hill-

[7] Is it possible that Mr. Beebe's position is homosexual as well as doctrinal? "Girls like Lucy were charming to look at, but Mr. Beebe was, from rather profound reasons, somewhat chilly in his attitude towards the other sex, and preferred to be interested rather than enthralled." (*ibid.*, p. 57)

side near Fiesole: "The silence of life had been broken by Miss Bartlett, who stood brown against the view." (p. 110) And much later, after George has kissed Lucy again, Charlotte silently presides over a scene in which Lucy, bewildered and angry, demands that George never see her again.

Before the end, however, Charlotte unexpectedly betrays a change of heart. Just as Mr. Beebe turns out to be less tolerant than we expected, Charlotte suddenly appears more so; she overrules his desire to keep Lucy from Mr. Emerson in the rectory, thus providing Lucy with the occasion for recognizing her love for George. The reversal, like Mr. Beebe's, adds a hint of complexity to an otherwise flat character, but it is not at all inconsistent with the novel's theme. If Charlotte has really wanted George and Lucy to marry, as George believes, it is because she is "not withered up all through" (p. 318)—because, that is, she retains a human spark which religion and society have not yet snuffed out.

Cecil, though he has nothing to say on the subject of religion, is clearly the product of a "Christian" milieu. His snobbery and bookishness are personal traits, but they go to make up an asceticism as rigid as Mr. Beebe's. The very first description of him makes this clear:

"He was mediæval. Like a Gothic statue. Tall and refined, with shoulders that seemed braced square by an effort of the will, and a head that was tilted a little higher than the usual level of vision, he resembled those fastidious saints who guard the portals of a French cathedral. Well educated, well endowed, and not deficient physically, he remained in the grip of a certain devil whom the modern world knows as self-consciousness, and whom the mediæval, with dimmer vision, worshipped as asceticism." (p. 136)

This image of Cecil as a medieval figure is preserved throughout the book; the last chapter, in which George and Lucy are seen together in an earthly paradise that Cecil would have found disgusting, is entitled "The End of the Middle Ages."

Unlike George, who is so unchivalrous that he enjoys beating Lucy at tennis, Cecil is punctiliously courteous to every woman; "The only relationship which Cecil conceived was feudal: that of protector and protected." (p. 235) In this he agrees with Charlotte, who tells Lucy that woman's role is not to participate in things but to exercise influence "by means of tact and a spotless name." (p. 67)

Forster of course regards this theory as pure cant. It is sweet, he says, to be chivalrous to one's wife when she has cooked the dinner well, "But alas! the creature grows degenerate. In her heart also there are springing up strange desires." (p. 68) The so-called Eternal Woman begins to feel a need to experience the world directly as her transitory self; she is a sentient, curious person, not a symbol of purity. Forster believes in absolute sexual equality, though not, incidentally, in "emancipation" as a way of life. The "emancipated" woman in A Room With a View, Miss Lavish, is a lady novelist whose efforts at daring produce only a fidgety romanticism. It is worth remembering that Lucy, who finally embodies Forster's idea of the happy modern woman, is last seen in the act of mending her husband's socks.

What Forster does want for woman is equality within a relationship of passionate love. This is what Lucy seems to obtain with George, who is aware of the overbearing tendency in his own temper and is determined to keep it in check (see p. 254). The marriage promises to be successful at least as long as the partners share a tenderness springing directly from physical love. "Passion is sanity" (p. 298), as Mr. Emerson declares; or again, "love is of the body; not the body, but of the body." (p. 307) Lucy by the end of the novel has learned what Rickie Elliot tried to learn and what Caroline Abbott and Philip Herriton were shown in Monteriano. Mr. Emerson's philosophy has triumphed: "He had robbed the body of its taint, the world's taunts of their sting; he had shown her the holiness of direct desire." (p. 311)

The moral of A *Room With a View*, then, is utterly simple: throw away your etiquette book and listen to your heart. The point is made with even less qualification than in *Where Angels Fear to Tread*, where Lilia's fate reminds us that the heart, too, can be mistaken. Like the earlier novel, A *Room With a View* gets its complexity not from theme but from comic tangles and the interpenetration of "rhythms." Many of the same devices, indeed, are carried over. In both novels the Italian countryside has symbolic value. The violets of passion outside Monteriano reappear on the hillside where George and Lucy first embrace: "Violets ran down in rivulets and streams and cataracts. . . ." (p. 110) This terrace of flowers, explains Forster, "was the well-head, the primal source whence beauty gushed out to water the earth" (p. 110), an image of obvious sexual meaning. In subsequent chapters Lucy associates the Emersons with violets, though she cannot remember why; Charlotte recalls that the carriage driver who brought Lucy to George had a violet between his teeth (p. 223); and flowers in general are in evidence when passion is in question.[8]

In both novels, too, the passage from spring to late autumn has an emblematic meaning. In the Italian sunshine passion is always imminent, but the threat of cold moralism becomes more oppressive as winter approaches. Toward the end of A *Room With a View*, while Lucy seems on the brink of permanent spinsterhood, the blustering weather reflects her danger. Windy Corner, her home, lies like "a beacon in the roaring tides of darkness." (p. 288) Lucy herself is so confused that she fears confidences, "for they might lead to self-knowledge and to that king of terrors—Light." (p. 291) The reader is hardly aware that the first of these images has a physical basis, the

---

[8] The same device appears in *The Longest Journey* with these overtones. When the elder Mr. Elliot is deserted by his passionate wife, he becomes aware that his drawing-room is "littered with sweet-peas. Their colour got on his nerves. . . . He tried to pick them up, and they escaped. He trod them underfoot, and they multiplied and danced in the triumph of summer like a thousand butterflies." (*The Longest Journey*, p. 269)

stormy weather, while the second does not. When Lucy is rescued she is both metaphorically and literally eligible to return to the Italian spring, where we find her at the end. Forster has worked the pathetic fallacy for all it is worth.

Typical of Forster's ingenuity with rhythms in this novel is his handling of the parallel images of music and water. When Mr. Beebe predicts of Lucy that "the water-tight compartments in her will break down, and music and life will mingle" (p. 144), he is joining two elaborate sets of metaphors. Lucy's playing of Beethoven sonatas, expressing passion and "Victory" rather than technical skill (see, for example, pp. 52f.), becomes equated with her self-fulfillment. When, for example, she ventures into the streets of Florence, half-hoping to meet someone like George, Mr. Beebe explains disapprovingly, "I put it down to too much Beethoven." (p. 66) When she does find George and hears him declare fervently, "I shall want to live, I say," Lucy "contemplated the River Arno, whose roar was suggesting some unexpected melody to her ears." (p. 76)[9] And at the very end, when the newlyweds have heard a song that "announced passion requited, love attained," the sound of the song becomes replaced by that of the Arno, "bearing down the snows of winter into the Mediterranean." (p. 318)[10]

As in *Where Angels Fear to Tread*, the scenes of climactic import tend to bind up the rhythms that run separately through the rest of the novel. The murder-scene in the Piazza Signoria is such an occasion; it is Lucy's introduction to violence and drama, to the passionate self she has not yet recognized. The most obvious symbol here is a photograph of Botticelli's "Birth

[9] Cf. Rickie's feeling at the moment of his discovering sexual passion: "Music flowed past him like a river. He stood at the springs of creation and heard the primeval monotony." (*The Longest Journey*, p. 52)

[10] One might also mention the use of water imagery to play upon the idea of true and false baptism. George has not had a Christian baptism, but he gets a pagan one in a mysterious pool near Windy Corner, where his worldly salvation is to be effected; and we may recall, when we find George immersed in this rite, that on the Fiesole hillside he had looked "like a swimmer who prepares." (*ibid.*, p. 110)

of Venus" which Lucy carries until it becomes bloodied and is dropped in the Arno by George.[11] Love and death, the realities cloaked by suburban religion, are emblematically joined, and the link is strengthened by the dying man's turning to Lucy "as if he had an important message for her." (p. 70) The message would seem to be that it is better to bring your passion out, even if it is murderous, than to remain unaware of its presence. When the driver on the Fiesole picnic conducts Lucy to George, Forster comments: "He alone had interpreted the message that Lucy had received five days before from the lips of a dying man." (p. 112)

There is, of course, no pretense of novelistic plausibility in devices of this sort. The carriage-driver's "interpretation" of words he never heard is purely a thematic gloss on Forster's part, a little nudge and wink at the reader. And, in a broader sense, the whole of A Room With a View is in the grip of Forster's preoccupation with theme. The scenery, the weather, the minor characters, and the apparent chances of plot are as rigidly governed by theme as in any novel by Henry James. It is certainly wrong to say of A Room With a View, as H. J. Oliver says of all Forster's novels, that its plot fights a losing battle with its characters.[12] Both plot and characters are mastered by Forster's desire to point a psychological moral. When George, for example, appears from nowhere to catch the fainting Lucy at the murder-scene, when the two of them are suddenly face to face on the hillside, and when they meet again at Windy Corner, we do not imagine that we are witnessing a series of realistic coincidences. On every occasion Lucy's passion *demands* that George appear; he is conjured up by her need of him. It is in this spirit, too, that Philip encounters Gino at the opera in *Where Angels Fear to Tread*. In these novels Forster is liberally indulging the dramatist's prerogative of seeing

[11] An analysis of the mythological aspects of this scene is given on pp. 132ff. below.

[12] See *The Art of E. M. Forster* (London and New York, 1960), p. 17.

that his events of plot work harmoniously with his gradual unraveling of theme.

The technical virtuosity of the Italian novels is bound together with their final narrowness of appeal. It is not that Forster resorts to improbable devices of plot—one could find the same practice in any of the other novels as well—but that the universe suggested by either of these works is no larger than the plot it contains. *Where Angels Fear to Tread* and *A Room With a View* are delightful books, but they do not attempt to touch us deeply or to recast our idea of the world's meaning. Their success, despite the bitter catastrophe in *Where Angels Fear to Tread,* is comic success; and Forster's career was to bring him a broader and more difficult mode of success in his two final novels.

Seven

THE COMIC SPIRIT

Forster's preoccupation as an artist, as we saw in *The Longest Journey*, has been with finding a viable symbolism. The symbolist wants to see universality and timelessness within his temporal experience, but he runs the risk of shallowness when this desire presses him too urgently. He must learn to "immortalize" only those moments in which the real world is naturally suffused with meaning. The trouble with Rickie Elliot's short stories, and equally with Forster's own, is an overbalance of meaningfulness at the expense of represented life—a preponderance of "unearned" symbolism. That this imperfection is less conspicuous in Forster's novels is largely due, I think, to the operation of a contrary feeling, his sense of the comic. Comedy provides the counterweight to keep the symbolist from slipping too far toward allegory; it continually refreshes his awareness of the world's intractability to private patterns of meaning.

In saying this I do not mean that comedy and symbolism, taken as literary methods, are opposites. Forster's Italian novels, with their purposeful selectivity of detail and their almost geometrical structure, are also highly comic; the recurrent symbols or rhythms can appear with equal plausibility in scenes of tragedy and of farce. This is made possible, however, by the fact that Forster's sense of irony governs the world of these novels. To a great extent the meaning he wants to create is ironic meaning; the significant moments are usually the ones that confound our surface expectations and those of the comically wrong-headed characters. A fictional world of this kind is patently artificial, for its details are chosen for their usefulness to the author's practical jokes. There is no urgency here to the characters' task of extracting "symbolic moments" from the chaotic world, for the represented world is not chaotic at all; it has already been severely trimmed to suit the purpose of the plot.

The opposition between symbolism and comedy pertains rather to the author's own search for meaning. If he is a humanist in the sense we have described—a man who disbelieves in all authority and order not verified by himself—he will be tempted to *perceive* the world in terms of his private values in order to protect himself from total disorder. As an artist he must reject this impulse; his symbolism has communicative power only insofar as it is grounded in the objective world known to his readers. The comic mode of vision is thus a helpful restraint upon the writer's zeal for meaning. In reminding him that there will be cakes and ale whether we accept his values or not, comedy insures him against facile self-importance and obscurantism.

This checks-and-balances notion of the writer's mind is the keynote of *Aspects of the Novel.* Forster's position on every question of theory is a middle one, involving a vital balance between extremes that threaten to "tyrannize" the novel. A novel should exist simultaneously in a world of time and a world of value, without giving itself wholly to either measure. It must be "sogged with humanity" (*Aspects of the Novel*, p. 43), but must possess formal unity. It must be beautiful without aiming at beauty; impressive, but never at the expense of truthfulness. Pattern is desirable, but not beyond the point where it begins to restrict "the immense richness of material which life provides." (p. 233) And a great part of this richness, for Forster, is unavailable to logical categories; it falls under the heading of "muddle," and is hence perceivable only by a sense of the incongruous. For this reason the "charmed stagnation" of *Tristram Shandy* is more congenial to Forster's taste than the relentless purposefulness of *The Ambassadors.* "The army of unutterable muddle" (p. 164) lies behind Sterne's masterpiece and provides its appeal. Or again, though Forster admires "prophetic" works like *Billy Budd*, he regrets that they require a suspension of the sense of humor (p. 211), for a sense of humor is needed to round out any vision of life, however glorious or intense it may be.

Forster's respect for muddle may help us to see the limitations of a fictional technique that he employs in most of his allegorical tales but generally eschews in his novels, namely, fantasy. Fantasy is, in Forster's definition, the "muddling up the actual and the impossible until the reader isn't sure which is which." (*Two Cheers*, p. 222) It consists of violating the conventions of plausibility without wholly dismissing them, so that the reader must take up two problematical views of reality instead of a single unquestioned one. The peculiar advantage of this technique (as of fantasy in its psychoanalytical meaning) is that it frees the writer from being strictly accountable to a world of distasteful facts. His wish for a more congenial order is projected onto an otherwise realistic narrative, thus sparing him a hopeless antagonism to his subject-matter. Though Forster wrings comic effects from his use of fantasy,[1] the technique is obviously not a tool of the comic spirit as I have defined it. Fantasy, we might say, is symbolism that has seized control of reality; it is the extreme luxury of self-indulgence which the true symbolist will try to avoid. In many of his tales Forster uses fantasy to manifest his belief in freedom and passion—in the typical situation a comically inhibited character is confronted with an ideally "free" world which he fails to comprehend—but the technique itself suggests an inflexible dogmatism of attitude. Since it undermines plausibility, we are not surprised to find that it plays only a minor part in Forster's relatively realistic longer fiction.[2]

[1] See, e.g., "The Story of a Panic," "The Other Side of the Hedge," "The Celestial Omnibus," and "The Curate's Friend," in the *Collected Tales*. Each of these stories embodies a sweeping criticism of accepted institutions or ideas, but each can remain good-humored because the satirized world is not the only one available.

[2] Forster does occasionally create a vague atmosphere of fantasy in his novels when he wants to suggest that the realm of value is asserting its claims over drab temporality. In *A Room With a View* this is the case in the murder-scene and in the dreamlike conclusion to the Fiesole episode,

Forster's sense of muddle, his willingness to admit violations and absurdities into his moral universe, is really quite opposite in spirit to his use of fantasy. It is one thing to produce effects of muddle by thwarting the expectations of narrow-minded characters—fantasy is well suited for this—but something else again to allow one's own values to be softened or qualified by a feeling for comedy. As a creator of fantasy Forster aligns himself with the Swift of *Gulliver's Travels* and the Butler of *Erewhon*: that is, with contrivers of schematic machinery for satirizing attitudes that are opposite to their own. His writing is also distinguished, however, by comedy in the restraining, self-critical sense. Like the Butler of *The Way of All Flesh*, Forster usually manages to satirize intolerant people without losing his characteristic modesty and nonchalance; he does not fall into the tone of the saint or the misanthrope. I return to Butler because Forster has confessed to a strong temperamental sympathy with him—not only with his common sense and intelligence, but with his good temper, graciousness, and "willingness to abandon any moral standard at a pinch." (*Two Cheers*, p. 221) This last quality suggests a healthy respect for the comic discrepancy between black-and-white values and the actual complexity and unpredictability of experience. Butler's influence on Forster, which was considerable,[3] was perhaps nowhere so great as in

---

and we may regard the theoretical presence of "ghosts" in *Howards End* and *A Passage to India* in a similar light. However far he may drift toward fantasy, though, Forster the novelist always remains anchored to the familiar and the tangible.

[3] Forster's specific borrowings from Butler, as well as some general similarities of opinion, are listed by Lee Elbert Holt, "E. M. Forster and Samuel Butler," PMLA, LXI (September 1946), 804-819. After Holt's article appeared, Forster produced an essay on Butler in which he confirmed the deep influence of Butler's eclecticism, and noted that he lectured on Butler "somewhere about 1910" and had contracted to write a book about him when the war broke out. Butler, he summarizes, "stands for the undogmatic outlook, for tolerance, good temper, good taste, empiricism, and reasonableness." See Forster, "The Legacy of Samuel Butler," *The Listener*, XLVII (June 12, 1952), 955f.

helping to fix his dominant attitude of self-belittlement, his application of comic irony to his own position as a moralist.

We can best describe the operation of the comic spirit in Forster's novels if we place him beside Jane Austen, his favorite novelist. As in her works, Forster's comedy is usually generated by ironic contrasts between what is superficially "proper" and what is truly reasonable. Characters like Cecil Vyse and Jane Austen's Mr. Collins are figures of fun because they lack self-knowledge; though Lucy Honeychurch and Elizabeth Bennett do not hesitate to tell us what to think of these stuffy gentlemen, the real satire is conveyed through verbal ironies within a narrow social context. And our standard of comic judgment in both cases is not a Puritanical concern for rectitude but simply an Augustan love of good sense. When the author has succeeded in exposing all the pride and prejudice, not only in these flagrant cases but also in the reformable central characters, the social structure remains intact. We have not been persuaded that family, class, and nation are bad, but that in order to live comfortably with these institutions one must see the modesty of one's place in the total scheme. Elizabeth Bennett, for all her caustic railing against hypocrisy, finally takes her privileged place in the social world, and so in a lesser degree does Lucy Honeychurch; the self-knowledge that has made them aware of their affections also tells them not to expand their revolt to Swiftian dimensions.

Where Forster's comedy chiefly differs from Jane Austen's is in the acceleration of its witty reversals, the greater density of thematic irony, and the greater freedom with which Forster moves his focus from the world of his characters to that of general human nature. The "double vision" that Lowes Dickinson found in his friend's work, and which James McConkey wisely takes as his starting-point in discussing Forster, is exercised almost incessantly. For illustration, let us see how the Fiesole outing in A Room With a View draws to its climax. Jane Austen would never offer us such an episode of complex disorder as this one; we seem to be closer to the world of Fielding or of Smollett. Neither Fielding nor Smollett, however, would press so much thematic meaning from his scene. In Forster the comic chaos is only apparent, for underneath it there always runs a discernible thread of logic, a reason in madness, that leads us straight to Forster's moral position.

The trip to Fiesole, we remember, culminates in the first kiss between George and Lucy, a "good" result in terms of the total plot of *A Room With a View*. It is introduced, however, by a series of comic mistakes, confusions, and petty social grudges among the English characters on the outing, who pride themselves on their national virtues of self-control and fair play. The broad irony of the sequence of events is obvious: the blunt and unsociable George Emerson will introduce Lucy to the possible harmony of her inward life, her true self, after the specious harmony of "society" has broken down. The elder Mr. Emerson helpfully states the theme, "Non fate guerra al Maggio," and adds, after his free translation of Lorenzo's line is pedantically contested by the Reverend Eager, "Do you suppose there's any difference between Spring in nature and Spring in man?" (*A Room With a View*, pp. 103f.) The day's voyage into the blooming Italian spring, against which the inhibited characters try unsuccessfully to "make war," brings Lucy and George to their own personal springtime of emotion. Through several patently symbolic devices, including the amorous sporting of a carriage driver and his sweetheart whom Forster calls "Phaethon" and "Persephone," Forster ensures that even the most obtuse reader will see the real drift of the scene.

What makes this episode distinctively Forsterian, however, is not simply its thematic weight but the multiplicity of its social ironies, which lead causally to the "celestial irony" (p. 97) of George and Lucy's encounter. The prospective lovers are together on this day only because the Reverend Beebe, who considers himself more "advanced" than the equally provincial Reverend Eager, has invited the Emersons without the latter's knowledge. The conversation during the drive consists of such appropriate remarks as Mr. Eager's observation that English tourists in Italy seem "quite unconscious of anything that is outside Baedeker," and the timidly adventuresome Miss Lavish's agreement that "the narrowness and superficiality of the Anglo-Saxon tourist is nothing less than a menace." (p. 98) A few moments later the same Mr. Eager is found berating the carriage driver for his loose morals while Miss Lavish is heroically trying to take a bohemian view of the case. The driver, with seeming implausibility, appeals to Lucy for support; like the murder-victim in the Piazza Signoria, he seems to be endowed with a special knowledge of her inner life. When "Persephone" has been exiled over Mr. Emerson's protests and the two carriages have arrived at their destination, the ironies of plot begin to quicken. Social antagonisms cause the party to split into three groups and then into stray individuals. Lucy, for instance, is set apart with Miss Lavish and Charlotte, but feels obliged to leave them when a fuss is made over the distribution of two mackintosh ground-cloths among the three ladies. The petty machinery of social form malfunctions so completely that Lucy is free to meet George unchaperoned.

Lucy, however, does not know that she wants to find George; she goes off in search of the two clergymen. In halting Italian she asks the carriage driver where the two "buoni uomini" can be found. The driver, who has been given a cigar by the *simpatici* Emersons, understands perfectly; he leads her straight to George. Lest we miss the implication that this is Lucy's buried wish, Forster now heightens the air of hidden meaningfulness in his narrative. Italians, he says, "are born knowing the way"; finding the right people is "a gift from God." (p. 108) From this point on Lucy increasingly rejoices in the contagious "influence of the Spring," until, when she is about to find George, Forster resumes the novel's central pun: "The view was forming at last." (p. 109) As Lucy stumbles into the bed of violets where George is waiting, the driver calls out *in English*: "Courage!

Courage and love" (p. 110), suggesting to us, as a last turn of irony, that Lucy's fortunate inability to communicate her surface meaning to him has been due to her tourist's grasp of the Italian language. Had she been more articulate, like the Reverend Eager and Miss Lavish, or less so, necessitating a conversation in English, she might not have been led to George. Altogether, Forster has arranged things so that his thematically inevitable climax is produced through a quick series of trivial comic surprises—each of which, however, is realistically justifiable in terms of the personalities involved. I can think of no other novelist who unravels his strands of social irony with such deft rapidity and complexity as this.

However believable any one of Forster's coincidences of plot may be, the hand of the puppet-master is clearly in view above his "meaningful" scenes of comedy. The Italian novels are so rigidly governed by thematic irony that their plots give a total effect of fantasy; we find ourselves in a world where error is always punished with ironic appropriateness. And this fact may suggest the name of another novelist whose influence on Forster seems hardly less important than Butler's or Jane Austen's. I am thinking of George Meredith, whose popular theory of comedy seems to be, if anything, more relevant to Forster's novels than to Meredith's own. Meredith insisted that the province of comedy was quite different from that of ordinary, plausible realism:

"Comedy is a game played to throw reflections upon social life, and it deals with human nature in the drawing-room of civilized men and women, where we have no dust of the struggling outer world, no mire, no violent crashes, to make the correctness of the representation convincing. Credulity is not wooed through the impressionable senses; nor have we recourse to the small circular glow of the watch-maker's eye to raise in bright relief minutest grains of evidence for the routing of incredulity. The comic spirit conceives a definite situation for a number of characters, and rejects all accessories in the exclusive pursuit of them and their speech. For being a spirit, he hunts the spirit in men; vision and ardor constitute his merit; he has not a thought of persuading you to believe in him."[4]

Instead of recording things as they are, Meredith's comic spirit focuses on human egoism and sees that it is justly punished. The comic plot assumes the function of a moral scourge, a purposeful agent of retribution against all forms of self-importance. And this can be said equally of Forster's own plots, particularly the early ones. Each of them enforces the proverb from Ecclesiastes that Anthony Failing expands to read, "Cast bitter bread upon the waters, and after many days it really will come back to you." (*The Longest Journey*, p. 157)

It is in the gentleness and impartiality of his comic spirit that Forster is more Meredithian than Meredith. In his famous *Essay on Comedy* Meredith laid special stress on the necessity for "a most subtle delicacy"[5] in the comic writer. His laughter must be both thoughtful and polite: neither charged with pathos like the humorist's nor barbed with malice like the satirist's. True comedy, for Meredith, involves the reader and even the author in the follies it exposes; as a tool of "clear reason" and common sense, it avoids the note of contempt that would place its user beyond comic criticism himself. "You may estimate your capacity for Comic perception," says Meredith, "by being able to detect the ridicule of them you love, without loving them less: and more by being able to see yourself somewhat ridiculous in dear eyes, and accepting the correction their image of you proposes."[6] It is very questionable, however, whether Meredith can pass his own test of objectivity. No reader of *The Egoist* can fail to sense the vengeful scorn that is heaped on the comic victim, Willoughby Patterne, and we search in vain through Meredith's novels for evidence that the author could laugh urbanely at himself. Forster, in contrast, remains

---

[4] George Meredith, *The Egoist* (New York, 1951), p. 3.
[5] George Meredith, *Miscellaneous Prose* (New York, 1910), p. 3.
[6] *ibid.*, p. 41.

both tolerant and affectionate toward his characters with "un-developed hearts." His politeness, instead of being a surface manner which checks a savage indignation, is intrinsic to his benevolent and self-critical approach to human nature.

The fact remains, however, that Forster's early plots are closely bound to the Meredithian formula of thwarting egoism. The role of Monteriano in *Where Angels Fear to Tread* is to administer comic justice to the English egoists. Egoism, in Meredith's terms, covers all forms of pretense and self-deception; not only Harriet Herriton, but also Philip, Caroline, and Lilia are tainted with egoism, for each is partly blind to his own nature. Philip and Caroline, the most flexible characters, are chastened and enlightened in the course of the plot. They are brought sharply against the truth of their desires and limitations, and they have to conclude that the world is larger and more complicated than they once thought. Lilia, whose susceptibility to infatuation stems from an unawareness of anything beyond her immediate passions, must live out the prosaic reality of her "romantic" marriage and finally die in childbirth. It is not because she is romantic that she is punished—Forster surely agrees with Meredith that the comic spirit "is not opposed to romance"[7]—but because her grasp of reality is weakened by sentimentalism. Harriet, who lacks "the very slightest sense of the ludicrous" (*Where Angels Fear to Tread*, p. 102), suffers a nervous breakdown after her abortive kidnapping. She has not really learned anything, but she has been severely chastened for her pretense of moral superiority. And the fact that a sense of the comic is a sign of self-knowledge also lies behind the farcical opera scene, which, for all its boisterous foolishness, is offered to the reader as a highly significant occasion, a moment of transformation for Philip. It is his escape from egoism toward Mr. Failing's principle that "nonsense and beauty have close connections,—closer connections than Art will allow." (*The Longest Journey*, p. 139) Harriet's inability to stand the zany antics

---

[7] *The Egoist*, p. 5.

of the Italian opera audience is consistent with her later indifference to a father's love for his son, and is thus the sign of a cardinal flaw of character that must be avenged.

Meredith's comic formula is more overtly the basis for Forster's treatment of Cecil Vyse in *A Room With a View*. Cecil himself is a great fan of Meredith's, and he regards himself as the agent of Meredith's Comic Muse. "George Meredith's right," he announces, "the cause of Comedy and the cause of Truth are really the same." (*A Room With a View*, p. 180) Cecil, of course, is the egoist whose own machinations produce his downfall. By bringing the Emersons to Windy Corner "in the interests of the Comic Muse and of Truth" (*ibid.*, p. 182), he hastens Lucy's realization that George Emerson is the man she really loves.[8] It is significant, too, that Cecil's insensitivity to the ludicrous is directly involved in Lucy's awakening. His absence from the "baptism" scene at the woodside pool, where the idea of salvation is again involved in an episode of farce, is as meaningful as George's presence there, and it is Cecil's refusal to make an ass of himself by joining a tennis match that suddenly persuades Lucy how "absolutely intolerable" he is. (p. 257) The plot of *A Room With a View* rescues Lucy herself from the form of egoism to which Charlotte Bartlett has already succumbed, that of setting herself above the vulgarity of sexual love.

In *The Longest Journey* we have a more complex and more serious novel, but one which nonetheless punishes its egoists *à la* Meredith. Rickie suffers for his effort to repudiate his physical nature, and Herbert and Agnes are rebuffed for their humorless self-importance. Mrs. Failing, it is true, seems to be spared by the Comic Muse, but her life is already devoid of comforting

---

[8] At this point in his career Forster is unabashedly taking the role of Comic Muse himself. "The Comic Muse," he writes, "though able to look after her own interests, did not disdain the assistance of Mr. Vyse. His idea of bringing the Emersons to Windy Corner struck her as decidedly good, and she carried through the negotiations without a hitch." (*A Room With a View*, p. 183)

illusions. *The Longest Journey* also takes up another of Meredith's comic ideas, that of the "hero" as it is ironically developed in *The Ordeal of Richard Feverel*. Stephen Wonham strikes Mrs. Failing as a hero, whose chief characteristics, she explains, "are infinite disregard for the feelings of others, plus general inability to understand them." (*The Longest Journey*, p. 121) As in Meredith's novel, this definition is of crucial importance, for in both cases (and in *The Egoist* as well) the resolution of the plot depends on whether a certain character is accepted in his "heroic" role or as an ordinary man. Stephen is idolized by Rickie in the same sense that Richard Feverel and Willoughby Patterne are idolized by Lucy Desborough and Laetitia Dale. Stephen is truly heroic, however, only by fits and starts, and when Rickie is forced to see his self-indulgent side, he turns against Stephen altogether. "To yield to temptation," Forster explains, "is not fatal for most of us. But it was the end of everything for a hero." (*The Longest Journey*, p. 318) Our last view of Stephen, however, refutes the opposite simplification, that of Mrs. Failing. The consummately normal Stephen, who shows himself to be an affectionate husband and father, has escaped from the categories of both hero and mock-hero.

In bringing his Meredithian theme to this conclusion Forster is not simply going beyond Meredith's pattern of inflicting vengeance on the false hero; he is also, it seems, questioning the legitimacy of that pattern. The Meredithian narrator who reserves for himself the luxury of exploding the myth of the hero becomes a character in Forster's novel (Mrs. Failing) and is subjected to Forster's criticism. Mrs. Failing's iconoclasm takes its place alongside Rickie's symbol-making as a falsification of the real world. I think we can see this, plus the fate of the Meredithian humorist Cecil in *A Room With a View*, as a kind of declaration of independence from Meredith's comic vogue. Forster makes free use of the current literary fashion of Meredithianism, but he is careful to show us that he is aware of its facility. By the time of *Aspects of the Novel*, certainly,

Forster was ready to dissociate himself from Meredith alto-gether: "What with the faking, what with the preaching, which was never agreeable and is now said to be hollow, and what with the home counties posing as the universe, it is no wonder Meredith now lies in the trough." (*Aspects of the Novel*, p. 136)

In view of this, we are not surprised to find that the idea of comic justice becomes progressively less relevant to our under-standing of Forster's two final novels. Forster retains his satiri-cal attitude toward egoists, of course, but his plots are not pri-marily concerned with exposing them. As moral questions be-come subordinate to questions about the ultimate meaning of human existence, the plot necessarily loses its function of super-intending private morality. Indeed, the very possibility of a Meredithian comic plot diminishes as Forster's total attitude toward life becomes more conspicuous. That attitude, we re-member, is one of extreme skepticism about the existence of a providential order. Such skepticism naturally precludes belief in a mechanical system of retribution against egoists; a novel based on such a system must be offered with a certain facetious flair. Now, however, we shall be turning to two novels that re-sume the effort, gingerly undertaken in *The Longest Journey*, to reflect the real poignancy of man's isolation from meaning. Forster's plots remain comic in that the characters are handled ironically, but his comic distance from them begins to take on a sober philosophical import—until, in *A Passage to India*, the comic vision accurately conveys Forster's view of human preten-sions in general. Forster remains comic, but in somewhat the same way that Chaucer is comic at the end of *Troilus and Cri-seyde*, where human tragedy is seen from the belittling perspec-tive of divine indifference to our imperfect and undignified lives.

HOWARDS END

In turning our attention to *Howards End* (1910), we reach a novel that puts into dramatic terms the liberal creed we examined at the end of Chapter Three. The framework of the novel is a series of antitheses between this liberalism and its opposite, a kind of blunt and humorless materialism; and the course of the plot, we might say, is an extended test of liberalism's ability to come to terms with its antagonist. Margaret Schlegel, the heroine, does not in any way reject the lofty notions with which she begins, but she does come to understand how difficult it is to preserve her ideals in the actual world. As is customary in Forster's novels, the triumph of an idea is purchased with a good deal of human anguish. Nevertheless, *Howards End* is the one novel in Forster's career that projects a reasonable hope for the survival of liberalism.

In the previous novels, liberal individualism wins out over "the world" or is beaten by it; in either case "the world" is felt only as a set of restrictions that can be dismissed or embraced simply through moral choice. Here, however, Forster has attempted to treat external reality as an imposing and permanent fact rather than as one term in a dialectical argument; there is no more possibility of "rejecting" the world in *Howards End* than there would be of rejecting the Alps or the Atlantic Ocean. And because Forster takes the trouble here to embody the anti-liberal forces in a complex and altogether human character, he has opened the possibility for a more realistic give-and-take— a marriage, in fact—between the supposed enemies. Henry Wilcox is somewhat awesome in his practical power, yet at the same time he is pitiful in his ignorance of private values. He needs the civilizing force of liberalism, just as liberalism needs his political and economic power. In the final, though perilously maintained, marriage between Henry and Margaret Schlegel, Forster voices his guarded hope that some place will actually be found for his own liberalism in modern industrial England.

This summary is not meant to reduce *Howards End* to allegory. But it is important to recognize that the book is schematic in its opposition of social and political values among the protagonists. If we look, first of all, at Helen and Margaret Schlegel, we find a joint incarnation of Forster's liberalism as we have defined it. English daughters of a naturalized German who turned against Germany's imperialism and materialism, they have been raised to feel that "any human being lies nearer to the unseen than any organization" (*Howards End*, p. 30)—and therefore, of course, that individuals outrank nations. Though weary of plans and "lines of action," they are concerned with politics: "They desired that public life should mirror whatever is good in the life within. Temperance, tolerance, and sexual equality were intelligible cries to them; whereas they did not follow our Forward Policy in Thibet with the keen attention that it merits, and would at times dismiss the whole British Empire with a puzzled, if reverent, sigh." (p. 28) Margaret Schlegel sees it as her duty "to be humble and kind, to go straight ahead, to love people rather than pity them, to remember the submerged." (p. 73) It is Forster's creed, and a simple one; but the action of *Howards End* springs from the fact that these principles are misunderstood and opposed by the busy world, that is, by the Wilcoxes.

Being "English to the backbone," the Wilcoxes are neither humble nor kind, nor do they "go straight ahead" morally, nor do they love outsiders—least of all those who have been "submerged" by the economic system that has provided their own affluence. They are "at best when serving on committees" (p. 98), which is to say that the personal side of life means very little to them. Or perhaps, as Helen Schlegel thinks, they realize its importance but are afraid of it because it reminds them of the hollowness of their self-importance (see p. 92). This self-importance is founded on their success in business, which in turn is interpreted as the result of "strength of character." Thus "Equality was nonsense, Votes for Women nonsense, Socialism nonsense, Art and Literature, except when conducive to strengthening the character, nonsense." (p. 24)

These are not harmless eccentricities, but grave and typical threats to the future of English culture, for the Wilcoxes and their kind are in control of industrialism, mechanization, urbanism—the forces to which all others seem fated to bow. Interestingly enough, the Wilcoxes represent a class that would certainly have voted Liberal before the decline of Gladstone's power, and for all we know they may be Liberals during the period covered by the novel. If they are, however, they belong among the Liberal imperialists from whom Chesterton was so anxious to distinguish himself. Having ridden to power on the crest of the Industrial Revolution, they are connected neither in spirit nor in fact to the gentle, rural, tradition-minded England that Forster loves. Their assumption of the role of landowners is, indeed, symptomatic of the late-nineteenth-century consolidation of the monied classes (landowners and industrialists together) in common opposition to the democratic movement.[1] It was a spurious alliance, and the Wilcoxes unwittingly expose its hollowness. The blundering destructiveness of Henry and especially of Charles Wilcox, his son, springs from the "panic and emptiness" of the purely acquisitive life, divorced from the liberalizing influences of the past.

Forster's pitiless anatomy of the Wilcoxes makes it impossible for us to sympathize with them; yet this, within certain rather narrow limits, is what the novel seems to be asking us to do. Although neither Forster nor his heroine is temperamentally equipped to love the Wilcoxes, both feel the necessity

[1] This alliance is clearly described by a contemporary: A. Hook, "Labour and Politics," *The Independent Review*, vi (1905), 197-205.

of trying, and the plot of the novel implies that at least some sort of modus vivendi can be reached. The case in favor of the Wilcoxes, which Forster presents as heartily as he can, rests on the fact that they are tenacious and practical. Margaret, who is more broadminded than the other Schlegels, formulates this positive argument in a pro-Wilcox moment: "Once past the rocks of emotion, they knew so well what to do, whom to send for; their hands were on all the ropes, they had grit as well as grittiness, and she valued grit enormously. They led a life that she could not attain to—the outer life of 'telegrams and anger' . . . To Margaret this life was to remain a real force. . . . It fostered such virtues as neatness, decision, and obedience, virtues of the second rank, no doubt, but they have formed our civilization. They form character, too; Margaret could not doubt it: they keep the soul from becoming sloppy. How dare Schlegels despise Wilcoxes, when it takes all sorts to make a world?" (pp. 103f.)

The tone of this passage is revelatory, particularly in the cliché at the end: both Margaret and Forster struggle unconvincingly to remind themselves of the Wilcox virtues. Those virtues, as Margaret knows too well, are basically unimportant if one is to place the highest value on spiritual things. It is also worth mentioning that the plot of *Howards End* eventually disproves a significant portion of the Wilcoxes' claim for recognition. Neither Henry nor Charles Wilcox has "character" in a moral sense, and their souls *are* sloppy if one means by that an inability to recognize the consequences of their actions. It is the Schlegels, and particularly Margaret, whose souls are clear and whose characters are strong. It is precisely Margaret's superior character, in fact, that enables her to forgive Henry for his moral blindness and to rescue him from despair at the end of the novel. Forster has not portioned out his real sympathy evenly enough to support the novel's schematic meaning.[2] De-

[2] D. H. Lawrence seems to have caught this false note. ". . . You *did* make a nearly deadly mistake," he wrote to Forster in 1922, "glorifying

spite his effort to give the Wilcoxes their due, the real point of *Howards End* is the familiar individualistic one. As Helen Schlegel puts it, "I know that personal relations are the real life, for ever and ever"—to which Margaret honestly replies, "Amen!" (p. 28) Margaret finally stays with Henry because she has seen how incomplete a world the Wilcoxes would build without the humanistic Schlegels to look after their souls.

Not the least important drawback of the Wilcoxes, in Forster's view, is their alliance with the power of urbanization. One of the central ironies of the novel is that the rural-minded Schlegels are for the most part constrained in London while the Wilcoxes, whose money has been made in cities, have been able to buy a chain of country estates and represent themselves as landowning aristocracy. Nomads at heart, the Wilcoxes are spiritually allied to the encroachment of cities onto the countryside. Howards End itself, standing in Southern Hertfordshire, is menaced by the expanding suburbs of London, but the Wilcoxes are indifferent to the danger, and still less, of course, do they appreciate the fact that it is really themselves who are rooting up England. They are restless, impatient, impervious to beauty; worshippers of the automobile, they ride across the hills and break them. The dust that they raise in speeding through country villages is only a foretaste of the urban soot that will shortly follow.

Forster's objections to London, though manifold, can be reduced to the charge that London frustrates the life of personal relations. The city refuses to lend itself to description in individual human terms: "One visualizes it as a tract of quivering grey, intelligent without purpose, and excitable without love; as

---

those *business* people in *Howard's* [sic] *End*. Business is no good." D. H. Lawrence, *Selected Literary Criticism*, ed. Anthony Beal (Melbourne, London, Toronto, 1955), p. 139. Lawrence, incidentally, who detested Bloomsbury, was not at all fond of Forster's art in general. See Angus Wilson, "A Conversation with E. M. Forster," *Encounter*, No. 50 (November 1957), 54.

a spirit that has altered before it can be chronicled; as a heart that certainly beats, but with no pulsation of humanity. It lies beyond everything: Nature, with all her cruelty, comes nearer to us than do these crowds of men. A friend explains himself: the earth is explicable—from her we came, and we must return to her. But who can explain Westminster Bridge Road or Liverpool Street in the morning—the city inhaling; or the same thoroughfares in the evening—the city exhaling her exhausted air? We reach in desperation beyond the fog, beyond the very stars, the voids of the universe are ransacked to justify the monster, and stamped with a human face. London is religion's opportunity—not the decorous religion of theologians, but anthropomorphic, crude. Yes, the continuous flow would be tolerable if a man of our own sort—not anyone pompous or tearful—were caring for us up in the sky." (p. 108)

We may note in passing that this connection of the city's inhumanity with the religious impulse illustrates Forster's idea that supernatural religion flourishes only where man's true relation to nature and other men has been frustrated. There is a form of religion that Forster does endorse in *Howards End*, but it is the this-worldly faith described in the "coinage" chapter of *The Longest Journey*—a faith that can be fully realized only in the countryside or among people who have been taught to feel the countryside's beneficent influence.

The autobiographical significance of Howards End—the association of it with Forster's own boyhood home—is explicitly stated in *Marianne Thornton*.[3] More obscure but more important is the nature of its effect upon the characters of the novel. Howards End is a repository of family tradition, and as such it has a mysterious ability to communicate the wisdom of its former residents to those who are willing to listen. Mrs. Ruth Wilcox, who was born there, has inherited this instinctive lore: "She seemed to belong not to the young people and their motor,

[3] See *Marianne Thornton*, p. 301.

but to the house, and to the tree that overshadowed it. One knew that she worshipped the past, and that the instinctive wisdom the past can alone bestow had descended upon her—the wisdom to which we give the clumsy name of aristocracy. Highborn she might not be. But assuredly she cared about her ancestors, and let them help her." (p. 22)

Like Mrs. Moore in *A Passage to India*, Mrs. Wilcox "means" more after her death than before it. Margaret Schlegel in particular feels her posthumous guidance, until Mrs. Wilcox has become virtually a patron deity for her. As Margaret says to Helen, "I feel that you and I and Henry are only fragments of that woman's mind. She knows everything. She is everything. She is the house, and the tree that leans over it. . . . I cannot believe that knowledge such as hers will perish with knowledge such as mine." (pp. 313f.) This semi-apotheosis raises more questions than it answers, but it does serve to merge the character of Mrs. Wilcox with that of Howards End, so that the two become interchangeable figures for the persistence of the past.

Mrs. Wilcox's role in the plot of *Howards End* is at once practical and highly symbolic. Although Margaret is not literally related to her, the two women are sisters in spirit. The dying Mrs. Wilcox declares Margaret the heir to Howards End, a bequest that is dismissed by the surviving Wilcoxes as the whim of a feverish brain. In one sense Margaret is temporarily cheated of what is hers, but in a deeper sense she is justly denied a role that she has not yet earned. The real bequest of Mrs. Wilcox is her nearly superhuman tolerance and self-control, the fruits of her continuity with the traditions of Howards End. Margaret possesses these virtues in theory but has not had to exercise them. Though believing utterly in what Mrs. Wilcox stands for, she must endure a period of trial and growth in which she will be tempted to exclude from her sympathy those who directly threaten her dearest values—the other Wilcoxes. By the end of the novel she will have become the new Mrs. Wilcox both in fact and in spirit, and thus will have resumed Ruth

Wilcox's interrupted program of civilizing those who might otherwise melt down the world.

It has become commonplace since Trilling's *E. M. Forster* to recognize that Howards End represents England itself and is the locus of a symbolic battle over England's destiny. It has another aspect, however, which has received little attention, yet which suggests a theme no less important than the political one. The house apparently stands for the integrated family life that was led there by Ruth Wilcox and is to be continued by Margaret. Howards End at its best—that is, when controlled by a woman of Mrs. Wilcox's type—represents an ideal, a standard, by which each of the novel's characters must be judged, and which Margaret herself must come to accept before she can replace Mrs. Wilcox. Like the novels that precede it, this one poses the question: how is life to be lived most fully? or, what is the proper relation between body and soul? Body and soul in the first three novels appear at first to be symbolically represented in geographical antitheses such as Sawston versus Monteriano, Cambridge versus Wiltshire, but the reader learns in each case that the place where the body is frankly accepted is also the best place for the development of the soul. In the present novel Howards End itself is the single emblem for Forster's ideal of harmony between the spiritual and the physical; to understand the meaning of the house is to dissolve the traditional opposition between these two elements.

This is seen most clearly in an episode during the period between the tenures of the two Mrs. Wilcoxes, when Howards End is deserted. Margaret, who has married the widowed Henry after a rather lengthy spinsterhood and is now thinking of reopening Howards End, visits her prospective home on a rainy, desolate day. She is struck by the beauty of the house, particularly in its relation to the land that provides its context; she regains the feeling of space and proportion that was upset by London and by Henry's jostling automobile. She wonders to herself whether Helen has been right in arguing that one must sacrifice important things to be a housewife: "She was not so sure. For instance, she would double her kingdom by opening the door that concealed the stairs." (p. 201) In other words, her life will be richer if she accepts both the "upstairs" and the "downstairs" of her new opportunities, the bedroom as well as the drawing room. Hitherto Margaret has lived in a world of books and plays and of close but merely "spiritual" friendships; here at Howards End she can live as a woman and a wife. There is room for her father's books—the life of the mind—in the library; there is room for Helen and her sisterly love; but there is also an upstairs, a physical life, which must be brought into concert with the rest.

Another way of formulating the same theme is to say that *Howards End* is a novel about reconciling the feminine with the masculine nature. The Schlegels, being dominantly feminine, run the risk of effeminacy; the masculine Wilcoxes verge on brutality.[4] Tibby Schlegel, the dilettantish brother of Margaret and Helen, is indeed effeminate, and Charles Wilcox is indeed brutal. Margaret and Henry, the most mature representatives of the two sides, fall in love and marry, thus providing at least a hypothetical union of opposites. Before she can make this marriage succeed, however, Margaret must realize the actual distance between Henry's nature and her own, and must adjust her hopes accordingly. As she tells Helen at the end, "people are far more different than is pretended. All over the world men and women are worrying because they cannot develop as they are supposed to develop. Here and there they have the matter out, and it comforts them." (p. 337) Margaret and Henry go through this ordeal themselves, and in "having the matter out" Margaret learns Forster's perennial lesson that physical love can be a cohesive force where mere rationality is insufficient. In the final stage of her development she has ceased to blame Henry for his peculiarly masculine callousness and has managed to accept him for what he is.

4 This antithesis is stated explicitly by Margaret, p. 44.

As usual in Forster's novels, the moral value sought by the hero or heroine is placed in relief by several characters who are conspicuously deficient in it. Helen Schlegel, though certainly a sympathetic figure throughout the book, lacks Margaret's and Mrs. Wilcox's moral flexibility, and she lacks it precisely because she is incapable of normal sexual love. She recognizes this incapacity—"I can only entice and be enticed" (p. 194), as she puts it—but she fails to see its restrictive effect on her judgments of the world. Her reason for preferring Margaret's love to that of any man involves a typical delusion among Forster's "incomplete" characters. "You and I have built up something real," she tells Margaret, "because it is purely spiritual. There's no veil of mystery over us. Unreality and mystery begin as soon as one touches the body." (p. 194)

This heresy against Forsterian dogma reveals an attitude comparable to Rickie Elliot's when he aspired to an unearthly symbolic relationship with his wife; and the result here is scarcely less disastrous than in *The Longest Journey*. Helen begins by "enticing" Paul Wilcox and immediately repenting of it, after which she becomes fanatically anti-Wilcox, that is, anti-male. This rigid stance leads directly to her tragedy. In resentment over Henry Wilcox's treatment of Leonard Bast, a young man whose low social position has placed him at the Wilcoxes' mercy, Helen spends a night with Leonard and conceives a child. Her desire to embody in a single act her opposition to Wilcoxism brings about a long period of unhappiness for herself and, in addition, nearly wrecks Margaret's resolution to put up with Henry. When Henry takes a priggish attitude toward her "sin," Helen almost persuades Margaret to join her crusade against masculinity. Margaret sequesters Helen in Howards End, insisting that Henry stay away: "A new feeling came over her; she was fighting for women against men. She did not care about rights, but if men came into Howards End, it should be over her body." (p. 290) This represents the triumph of Helen's narrow view, and, conversely, the rejection of Ruth Wilcox's ideal of harmony. It is only a momentary defeat, however; eventually even Helen reaches a sympathetic understanding of Margaret's heroic compromise. Though she can never love a man, she discovers that she can give her affection freely to her child. Margaret, in contrast, sincerely loves Henry but is not interested in children (see pp. 198f., 273), and the two sisters together, both living on at Howards End, finally compose an adequate substitute for Ruth Wilcox, the wife and mother combined.

Another character with an inadequate grasp of the interdependence of body and soul is Henry Wilcox. While Helen distrusts sex because it complicates life beyond her power of mastery, Henry distrusts it on religious grounds. Forster uses him to illustrate his well-known view about the psychological effects of asceticism: "Outwardly he was cheerful, reliable, and brave; but within, all had reverted to chaos, ruled, so far as it was ruled at all, by an incomplete asceticism. Whether as boy, husband, or widower, he had always the sneaking belief that bodily passion is bad, a belief that is desirable only when held passionately. Religion had confirmed him. The words that were read aloud on Sunday to him and to other respectable men were the words that had once kindled the souls of St. Catherine and St. Francis into a white-hot hatred of the carnal. He could not be as the saints and love the Infinite with a seraphic ardour, but he could be a little ashamed of loving a wife." (p. 186)

This furtive religiosity sits especially ill on Henry, who has been unfaithful to Ruth Wilcox with the present common-law wife of Leonard Bast, and who has never really applied religious standards in judgment of his own amours. A believer in sowing wild oats, he refuses to distinguish between unchastity and infidelity, that is, between technical "sin" and the violation of his wife's trust. The difference is a crucial one for Forster because of his faith in personal relations as opposed to abstract moral law: to harm another person is worse than to debauch oneself.[5] It is Henry's Christianity that prevents him from seeing this distinction, and it is also his Christianity that enables him to excuse his conduct as being typical of sinful mankind. And, of course, Forster does not expect us to miss the connection between Henry's infidelities and his embarrassment over loving his wife. A smattering of religion can make us ashamed of our bodies but it cannot make us less carnal; the part of Henry that seems out of place in his "pure" and "respectable" marriage finds expression in his affair with the appropriately "low" Jackie Bast.

Forster tells us explicitly that the Middle Ages have been Henry's only moral teacher (p. 259). In this light it is understandable that the other side of his sneaking prurience should be a chivalrous protectiveness toward women, like that of the "medieval" Cecil Vyse. Forster is always satirical about this superior gallantry; it is simply a means of denying the equality of the sexes, and hence of obstructing that true rapport between men and women which, Forster says, is an outcome of sex but is not to be confused with it. Henry and Helen are alike in their inability to find this relationship. What Forster says of Helen is largely true of Henry: "Helen forgot people. They were husks that had enclosed her emotion. She could pity, or sacrifice herself, or have instincts, but had she ever loved in the noblest way, where man and woman, having lost themselves in sex, desire to lose sex itself in comradeship?" (p. 311) Though they are different in every other way, Henry and Helen together are deprived of a full emotional and imaginative life because of their distorted understanding of sex.[6]

With these two important characters predisposed to a limited

[5] In this connection one is reminded of Mill's argument in *On Liberty* that society is justified in restraining personal action only when that action threatens the welfare of other people. Sharing Mill's disbelief in sin, Forster is led to a moral Utilitarianism basically similar to Mill's.

[6] Tibby Schlegel is another such character, and Forster's plot, in making Tibby's indifference to life an oblique cause of Leonard Bast's death (*Howards End*, pp. 310f.), underscores the moral importance of passion.

point of view, our attention falls centrally on Margaret, the most flexible and self-examining person in *Howards End*. Helen and Henry draw her in opposite directions, toward "spirituality" and sexual tenderness respectively. What finally saves her from Helen's exclusive feminism, however, is not so much Henry's appeal as her own conscientious desire to be truthful to her nature. "Few women," we are told, "had tried more earnestly to pierce the accretions in which body and soul are enwrapped." (p. 103) Margaret's investigations lead her, not surprisingly, to Forster's own conviction that there is a human mean where the artificial choice between asceticism and depravity disappears —a "tenderness that kills the Monk and the Beast at a single blow." (p. 220)

This is not to say that body and soul themselves are exposed as invalid categories; on the contrary, Margaret wants to subject herself to their opposite attractions. In resisting Helen's facile acquaintance "with reality and the absolute," Margaret thinks to herself: "The business man who assumes that this life is everything, and the mystic who asserts that it is nothing, fail, on this side and on that, to hit the truth. 'Yes, I see, dear; it's about halfway between,' Aunt Juley had hazarded in earlier years. No; truth, being alive, was not halfway between anything. It was only to be found by continuous excursions into either realm, and though proportion is the final secret, to espouse it at the outset is to insure sterility." (p. 195) The plot of *Howards End* forces these "continuous excursions" upon Margaret until she has actually arrived at the secret of proportion. As Howards End successfully connects nature with the human past and present, so Margaret, by accepting her desires and limitations, succeeds in reconciling the spiritual and physical sides of herself.

The imaginative wisdom that enables Margaret to draw this connection is also required for another important problem in *Howards End*, that of social responsibility. The center of dispute here is Leonard Bast, whose very name suggests his thematic role: he is the illegitimate offspring of the social system that has pampered both the Wilcoxes and the Schlegels. He is "at the extreme verge of gentility" (p. 45), neither starving nor quite respectable. Though he aspires to the Schlegels' degree of culture, he is inhibited by his consciousness of the abyss of poverty beneath him, and his efforts to "improve" himself are pathetically misdirected. He becomes, for the Schlegel sisters as well as for Forster, a symbol of the worst effects of modern capitalism, which encourages people like Leonard to be dissatisfied with their circumstances and at the same time frustrates their desire for recognition.

Leonard's very existence poses the question of what is to be done to improve the social structure, and the Schlegels use him as the locus of a rather frivolous debate on this subject early in the novel. But again, the plot of *Howards End* provides a more vivid and drastic working-out of the issue than is possible through mere argumentation. Leonard becomes involved in the lives of both Schlegels and Wilcoxes, and his symbolic role develops from the way he is treated by these representatives of other classes. Each of the other major characters must discover whether he can take Leonard into his field of vision without distorting the entire perspective. Each must decide, in other words, whether he can afford to acknowledge that his own well-being is founded on the intimidation and plundering of others who are less favored socially.

In a sense the Wilcoxes do recognize this; they take the Benthamite position that there will always be rich and poor, and that the market of free competition justly eliminates the weak and unworthy. It does not occur to them, however, that Leonard is poor because his grandparents were driven out of the countryside by the same economic force that has enriched the Wilcoxes themselves (see p. 237), and because Leonard himself, having been deprived of the life of the body, has been given no resources to cultivate the life of the spirit (see p. 115). Furthermore, Henry Wilcox has contributed personally to Leonard's degradation, first by "ruining" the woman who has subsequently attached herself to Leonard and helped to submerge him, and secondly by offering him a word of mistaken advice which persuades him to give up his job and thus become really destitute. These two facts converge when Leonard returns with Jacky to beg Henry for aid; Henry sees his ex-mistress, suspects blackmail, and turns his back on both of them. On one level it is merely a coincidence of plot that Henry and Jacky are already acquainted; but thematically it is not coincidental at all. Henry, the successful entrepreneur, has used the lower-class, relatively helpless Jacky for his pleasure and then abandoned her. Confronted with the image of his guilt—a guilt which is at once personal and social and economic—Henry characteristically places the blame on the abused party rather than on himself. He is blind to his actual and theoretical indebtedness to the Basts.

Margaret, in contrast, is quite sensitive to the interdependence of the various levels of society. While the supposedly realistic Henry converts every social question into terms of "character" and "backbone," the idealistic Margaret understands the primary importance of economic privilege. "You and I and the Wilcoxes," she tells her aunt, "stand upon money as upon islands." (p. 61) This awareness enables Margaret to see that her own opinions, including those about moral right and wrong, originate in her social background, and this in turn provides her with a charitable attitude toward those, such as Leonard, who live not upon islands of money but "below the sea." (p. 61) It is not a question of pretending that Leonard is superior in dignity because he is downtrodden; neither Margaret nor Forster believes that the poor are especially blessed. They see, rather, that Leonard's want of dignity has something to do with his circumstances; they pity him without glorifying him.

Once again, we find that Helen Schlegel has a blind spot similar to Henry's. Unlike Margaret, she does create a romanticized picture of the Leonard who might have existed if conditions had permitted: "A real man, who cared for adventure and beauty, who desired to live decently and pay his way, who could have travelled more gloriously through life than the Juggernaut car that was crushing him." (p. 316) Henry, of course, disagrees absolutely with this analysis, but his own is comparable in simplicity; as Helen exaggerates economic pressure, Henry exaggerates "character." Toward the end of the novel Helen comes to understand the mistake she has made about Leonard, and her explanation is incisive: "One isolates," she says. "I isolated Mr. Wilcox from the other forces that were pulling Leonard downhill." (p. 312) This is precisely what Henry has done with the element of "character"—a real factor in Leonard's submersion, but by no means the only one. Helen and Henry together are people who isolate and simplify rather than allowing their imaginations to play across a broad range of related circumstances. They fail to *connect*; and "Only connect . . . ," as every reader of *Howards End* will remember, is the motto on the title-page of the book.

It is not surprising, then, that the "panic and emptiness" behind the Wilcoxes' façade of importance (see, for example, pp. 26, 92, 235) assault Helen, too, when she learns of Margaret's engagement and again when she has slept with Leonard. (pp. 172, 313) Both the Wilcoxes and Helen are reluctant to come to grips with prosaic reality. Like Rickie Elliot and to a lesser extent like Cecil Vyse and Philip Herriton, they live in a world of make-believe which shuts out both ecstasy and tragedy, and which falls in ruins at the first intrusion of either. The dominant moral value of *Howards End*, as of *The Longest Journey*, is the ability to accept the actual world for what it is: to "live in fragments no longer," as Margaret puts it. (p. 187) Panic and emptiness are inherent in the human situation, and if one is not to be suddenly paralyzed by them he must recognize them from the first and somehow placate them. This, for Helen, is the meaning of Beethoven's Fifth Symphony: the "goblins" of panic and emptiness are deliberately evoked and then exorcised through the assertion of human order. In her own life, however, Helen is unable to cope with her doubts. Her semi-hysterical sympathy with Leonard, like Henry's obtuseness towards him, reflects the dangerously narrow limits of her sense of truth. Only Margaret, whose nature is firmly rooted in prosaic fact, can meet the central crisis of the novel and rescue the others from disillusion.

Margaret's redeeming virtue, the ability to "connect," operates on every level of action in *Howards End*. In her own psyche she resolves the antagonism between body and soul by accepting her role of wife in the fullest sense. In dealing with Leonard she connects the restrictive force of his background with his fundamental mediocrity; she does not explain one purely in terms of the other, but is able to see the two facts as discrete yet related. At the same time, she sees the connection between Leonard's poverty and her own wealth; she accepts a share of hereditary responsibility for his ill-treatment. Again, and in conspicuous contrast to the Wilcoxes, Margaret can connect the human past with the present and future. Her sense of tradition, centering on Howards End, is indistinguishable from the quiet strength of her moral nature. And, finally, in "connecting" herself to Henry Wilcox through marriage, she not only bridges the perilous gap between male and female, but symbolically marries her civilizing force to the power of modern England. In every case it is Forster's own humanistic faith, his belief in the value of individual love and tolerance, that sees Margaret through. And this faith, as we have noted in the other novels, expresses both a yearning for permanence and a realistic sense of limitation. Henry lacks it because he recognizes no boundaries to his selfhood; Helen lacks it because she secretly despises the real world; and Leonard lacks it because his class consciousness is too oppressive. Margaret is the heroine of *Howards End* not because she is the "best" character, but because she is the only one who can gauge the scope of her own power.

For all its moral consistency, however, we may be permitted to wonder whether *Howards End* is, as Lionel Trilling asserts, "undoubtedly Forster's masterpiece."[7] It is easy to agree that this novel "develops to the full the themes and attitudes of the early books," and that it shows "a more mature sense of responsibility";[8] but moral responsibility and aesthetic value are not the same thing. Indeed, in a writer whose sense of reality is so ironic as Forster's, one sometimes feels the effort to be "responsible" as an impediment to sincerity. What we have in *Howards End*, in my opinion, is a novel that tries schematically to qualify Forster's previously oversimplified antithesis between the inner and outer worlds. This, at any rate, is the task that Forster sets for Margaret Schlegel. But the more closely we scrutinize the Wilcoxes, the less convinced we are that Forster has been able to compromise his original feelings. The outer world remains alien—panic and emptiness, telegrams and anger, the mindless destruction of personal values. Margaret's "connection" with the Wilcoxes is merely diagrammatic. Her actual relationship to Henry at the end of the novel is more eloquent: having tamed him and demonstrated her indispensability to him, she is willing to nurse him in his helplessness. However eclectic and conciliatory Forster tries to be, however disinterestedly he reminds us of our dependence on society, his novel ends by crushing society on the altar of the private life.

This is to say that *Howards End*, in undertaking more than its predecessors, suffers from a greater strain between what is intended and what is sensed between the lines. Forster's misgivings about "the world," which are everpresent in his writing, are damaging here precisely because he has made such a bold effort to allay them. His plot must finally retreat to an unconvincingly "moral" ending—it must revert to comic justice, in other words —in order to be saved from disintegration. Thus we can speak of both development and failure in *Howards End*: development in

[7] *E. M. Forster*, p. 99.
[8] *ibid.*, p. 99.

that Forster has expanded his willingness to admit the prosaic outer world into his fiction, but failure in the task of truly reconciling this world with his own values. As Forster's art grows more realistic, his humanism is more clearly seen as an isolated phenomenon, a candle in the dark, until finally in A *Passage to India* we find ourselves peering uncertainly into the dark itself.

Nine

THE LIMITATIONS OF MYTHOLOGY

It is difficult, if not impossible, to speak of chronological "progress" among Forster's novels prior to *Howards End*. The dates of composition of the three earlier works overlap, and the differences of tone and theme among them seem to be controlled more by genre or intention than by Forster's growth as an artist. With *Howards End*, however, the stages of Forster's career begin to assume an intelligible order. Though his method of seeing the world is not perceptibly different, his art acquires a new seriousness of purpose, a new intricacy of plot and symbolism, a broadening of social and metaphysical reference. It now becomes possible to recognize not only a technical development, but also an extension of the total meaning of Forster's fictional universe. We can, in fact, see this extension of meaning within his handling of technical devices. The gradual disappearance of allusions to Greek mythology, for example, marks a growing independence from a certain current of shallow moralism that runs through the earlier novels. Forster's ideas about man and nature remain much the same, but his shift of method in presenting them reflects a radical change of emphasis.

Some orientation to the problem of interpreting Forster's use of mythology may be gotten from Nietzsche's famous distinction between the Apollonian and the Dionysian principles. The Dionysian, according to Nietzsche in *The Birth of Tragedy*, is the spirit that feels the oneness of all things, and which consequently shares in all the pain and ecstasy in the universe. Its Promethean seizure of forbidden experience quickly becomes unbearable and must be succeeded by the spirit of Apollonianism. The Apollonian is the *principium individuationis*; it recognizes forms, borders, and categories, and imposes the image of finite humanity upon the disorder of experience. As opposed to the Dionysian involvement in excess, the Apollonian insists on measure and morality; it substitutes the ideal of knowledge for that of participation. Tragedy, the highest of the arts, ideally transfixes experience at the moment when the Dionysian consciousness, tormented by its too-inclusive grasp of chaos, creates for itself an image-world in which its vision is "sorted out" into stage conflicts—just the moment at which the unbearable is made bearable. Art is doomed to sterility, for Nietzsche, unless it draws its Apollonian images from a Dionysian intoxication with the primal unity.

If we ask to what extent these two terms apply to Forster's English predecessors who borrowed Greek mythology, we find a general trend of Apollonianism. Among Romantic works, one thinks at once of Keats's *Hyperion*, which was meant to celebrate the dethronement of the Titans by a relatively gentle, lyre-strumming Apollo. And Shelley's *Prometheus Unbound*, while glorifying the rebellious Titans, is utterly Apollonian in spirit. Shelley's Prometheus is as far from Dionysus as his Jupiter is. The Shelleyan apotheosis of human reason, the triumph of good over evil, the humanization of nature are all foreign to Nietzsche's Prometheanism, which defies the gods from a self-immolating, not a self-improving, urge. Most of the Victorians are still further removed from Nietzsche's sense of the Dionysian. In Tennyson and Browning the myths become merely decoration for modern themes or occasions for the construction of psychological "characters." Matthew Arnold's classicism was more deeply felt but was equally free of Nietzschean frenzy. It was sweetness and light, not the brutal ecstasy of Dionysus, that Arnold looked for in the Greek nature, and his ideal was always the Apollonian one of *self*-cultivation.[1]

There are, however, certain Victorians who reveal the con-

[1] The foregoing paragraph is indebted to Douglas Bush, *Mythology and the Romantic Tradition in English Poetry* (Cambridge, Mass., 1937), *passim*.

trary spirit. Swinburne, though basically a humanist, dwelt on the erotic and sadistic elements that Nietzsche includes in the Dionysian, and was in fact a student of the ancient cult of Dionysus. Pater, too, was fascinated by the Dionysian. His semi-anthropological essay, "A Study of Dionysus," attempts to be objective about the cult but contains such implicit value-judgments as the following: "A type of second birth, from first to last, [Dionysus] opens, in his series of annual changes, for minds on the look-out for it, the hope of a possible analogy, between the resurrection of nature, and something else, as yet unrealised, reserved for human souls; and the beautiful, weeping creature, vexed by the wind, suffering, torn to pieces, and rejuve-nescent again at last . . . becomes an emblem or ideal of chasten-ing and purification, and of final victory through suffering."[2]

This is really Victorian ameliorism in disguise; as Pater con-fesses, he is referring only "to ethical culture, to the perfecting of the moral nature."[3] Yet elsewhere Pater shows a less tenden-tious understanding of the myth. In his imaginary portrait, "De-nys L'Auxerrois," he reincarnates the figure of Dionysus in a medieval French town. Denys (Dionysus) awakens the latent Dionysianism of the Christian villagers, who pass through the successive phases of the bacchant: exuberant joy, morbid sav-agery, and, finally, satiation and lethargy. It is unlikely that Pater intends us either to approve or disapprove of this sequence; he seems only to be dramatizing the idea that human nature in any age is susceptible to immersion in the Dionysian. Yet his story is suggestive in that it recognizes the sacrifices involved in Diony-sianism; Pater would seem to accept the Nietzschean point that true "harmony with nature" entails a rejection of the human norm, a subversion of rational morality.

The relevance of all this to Forster would seem at first to be nil. As an avowed humanist and apostle of reason, he is wary

[2] Walter Pater, Greek Studies; A Series of Essays (New York, 1894), pp. 44f.
[3] ibid., p. 44.

of emotional excesses. Tragedy is not his mode of seeing things;[4] and as for removing the veil of Maya and joining the totality of experience, A *Passage to India* tests the idea and finds it wanting. "Visions are supposed to entail profundity," he writes, "but—Wait till you get one, dear reader!"[5] In an age of cataclysms that might have satisfied even Nietzsche's appetite for the titanic and the barbaric, Forster has persistently argued for the Apollonian spirit of moderation. His intellectual ideals of tolerance, skepticism, and respect for factual truth form the essence of what Nietzsche stigmatized as Socratism.[6]

Forster's Cambridge training in classics, however, might encourage us to look for traces of Dionysianism in his work. It is unlikely that he remained unaware of a trend in Cambridge anthropology that was influencing the interpretation of literature at the turn of the century. J. G. Frazer's *The Golden Bough*, the first of whose twelve volumes appeared in 1890, vastly extended the concept of primitivism beyond the limits of aboriginal cultures. Drawing examples from both the modern and the ancient world, Frazer revealed a substructure of magical beliefs under even the most advanced societies. The relevance of this demonstration to classical studies is evident if we recall how suddenly Greek civilization blossomed; in W. K. C. Guthrie's words, "It had sprung at a bound from darkness into light."[7] As anthropologists began scrutinizing the classics for atavisms, so

---

[4] Witness, e.g., his attitude toward war. Writing in 1939, he asked: "Ought we not, at such a moment, to act as Wagnerian heroes and heroines, who are raised above themselves by the conviction that all is lost or that all can be saved, and stride singing into the flames?" (*Two Cheers*, p. 21) Nietzsche, for whom Wagner at one time represented the ideally tragic consciousness, would probably have replied in the affirmative. Forster, however, simply remarks with customary sobriety: "No one who debates whether he shall behave tragically can possibly be a tragic character." (*ibid.*, p. 21)

[5] A *Passage to India* (New York, 1924), p. 208.

[6] It should be added that Nietzsche admired these virtues, and even admired Socrates. It was the lack of a counterbalancing Dionysian expansiveness that made them disagreeable to him.

[7] W. K. C. Guthrie, *The Greeks and Their Gods* (London, 1950), p. 18.

classicists acquired a new respect for anthropology. Jane Harrison, herself a Cambridge scholar, was to recall that "we classical deaf-adders stopped our ears and closed our eyes; but at the mere sound of the magical words 'Golden Bough' the scales fell —we heard and understood."[8]

What the classicists understood was, among other things, that the Olympian deities were to be regarded no longer in the decorative, static, half-serious fashion that had been customary since Ovid. Rather, they were the survivors of a battle with an earlier and cruder religion. The point made by Nietzsche in *The Birth of Tragedy*, that Apollonian religion gains its impetus from an awareness of the Dionysian chaos that precedes it, was more or less corroborated.[9] And literary people were quick to see the application of Frazer's researches to psychology. When Gilbert Murray wrote that "there is hardly any horror of primitive superstition of which we cannot find some distant traces in our Greek record,"[10] he was adducing a reason for, not against, the study of Greek religion. The "dark gods" who recur in the pages of Joyce, Yeats, Lawrence, and Eliot are now personifications of unconscious human forces. The mysterious and often savage underside of man's nature became a major subject of modern art, and with it came a revitalized notion of the truth of the Greek myths.

Whether or not Forster felt this current, it is certain that his early stories show a distinct hospitality to the idea of Dionysianism. "The Story of a Panic" comes to mind at once in this connection. It deals with the transformation of a normal English

[8] Jane Ellen Harrison, *Reminiscences of a Student's Life* (London, 1925), p. 83.

[9] I gather that one of the fruits of recent anthropology, however, has been the discovery that the simple antithesis between the cults of Dionysus and Apollo is untenable. There is evidence, indeed, that at certain moments the two deities were considered identical. See W. K. C. Guthrie, *Orpheus and Greek Religion; A Study of the Orphic Movement* (London, 1952), pp. 43, 46, 218.

[10] Gilbert Murray, *Five Stages of Greek Religion* (New York, 1925), pp. 15f.

boy named Eustace into a disciple of "the great god Pan," who appears (or one of whose satyrs appears) to Eustace in the Italian countryside. The story is built around the comic misunderstanding that Eustace's fellow-Englishmen, including the narrator, display in trying to curb the new Eustace's activities. These include a delirious romp in the woods and a flow of rhetoric about "great forces and manifestations of nature":

"He spoke first of night and the stars and planets above his head, of the swarms of fire-flies below him, of the invisible sea below the fire-flies, of the great rocks covered with anemones and shells that were slumbering in the invisible sea. He spoke of the rivers and waterfalls, of the ripening bunches of grapes, of the smoking cone of Vesuvius and the hidden fire-channels that made the smoke, of the myriads of lizards who were lying curled up in the crannies of the sultry earth, of the showers of white rose-leaves that were tangled in his hair. And then he spoke of the rain and the wind by which all things are changed, of the air through which all things live, and of the woods in which all things can be hidden." (*Collected Tales*, pp. 28f.)

This is at least superficially similar to the Dionysian participation in all experience. It is significant, too, that Forster neglects to claim that Eustace has been morally improved by his new naturalness; although we are sympathetic with his escape from his staid countrymen, it is made clear that his Apollonian "character" has disintegrated. Insofar as the Dionysian equates freedom with wild excess, "The Story of a Panic" is Dionysian.

Less mythological, though similar in theme, is "The Other Side of the Hedge," which presents its hero with a choice between the ordinary temporal world and a timeless existence in which he can perceive "the magic song of nightingales, and the odour of invisible hay, and stars piercing the fading sky." (p. 48) Dionysian wildness is missing, but the story's logic is Nietzschean—an awareness of the unity of all things is granted only after the temporal, "Socratic" spirit has been abandoned. Then, too, there is "The Story of the Siren," an account of the destruction of two people who claim to have seen a siren and are considered mad by society. The moral of the story is obscure, but its frame, again, is a contrast between the workaday human world and a darker, mythic order of experience.

It is not difficult, however, to see that these stories are really in harmony with Forster's total ethical ideal. That ideal is the Apollonian one of proportion, but of *vital* proportion, between body and soul, passion and intellect. In his novels, particularly in *The Longest Journey* and *Howards End*, Forster has the leisure to bring his central characters to this balance by subjecting them to Margaret Schlegel's "continuous excursions into either realm." The short stories, on the other hand, must confine themselves to a single psychological reversal, and this usually means that only the first "excursion" toward a final harmony can be taken, namely, a confronting of the passionate side of one's nature. At bottom, Forster's tales rest on a rather conventional antithesis between naturalness and inhibition, paganism and suburban Christianity.

This antithesis is the key to interpreting several of his other tales. In "Other Kingdom," for example, the Apollo-Daphne myth is given a refreshing twist: the girl who becomes a tree is spared not from ravishment, but from the opposite, a life in which her senses would have been starved. Again, the faun who appears unexpectedly to the curate in "The Curate's Friend" is at once a representative of the spirit of the countryside and a mirror in which the curate and his fiancée can see their true selves—their selves in natural rather than otherworldly terms. And "The Road From Colonus" offers its aged hero the hope of "becoming a god" like Oedipus. Standing in a hollow tree, he feels himself accepted into the heart of nature for the first time, and, though his companions save his life by cajoling him away, we are plainly expected to sympathize with his original wish.

In each of these tales the Dionysian identification with nature points dimly ahead toward the Apollonian ideal of self-knowledge. Instead of losing all sense of relationship in empathy with the world-soul, Forster's characters begin to see *more* relationships than previously; they cherish their individuality more dearly. Forster himself, though he concurs with the Nietzschean view that man has a deep kinship with the forces of nature, recoils from any true commitment to the Dionysian. His paganism, like Pater's, refers "to ethical culture, to the perfecting of the moral nature." Between his attitude and Nietzsche's lies a gap as broad as that between skepticism and mysticism, comedy and tragedy, moderation and heedless revolt.

On the whole, then, Forster's use of mythology in his tales does not depart from the English Romantic tradition. We need not refer to the anthropologists to see parallels to his way of regarding the Greeks: it is implicit in Cambridge classicism of the 1890's and in the fashionable literature of that decade. We have already seen that his interest in Greek civilization, and specifically his admiration of its freedom from asceticism, closely follows the views of Lowes Dickinson; the Greek acceptance of passion within the ideal of proportion was one of the axioms of life at King's. And here again, the name of George Meredith suggests itself. Forster's morality of passion does not really go far beyond Meredith's belief in steering between the ascetic rocks and the sensual whirlpools. Forster is a little franker, a little more "psychological," but his early work still employs the Meredithian formula of cloaking ethical questions in the elegant garb of mythology. When Forster confesses in *Howards End* that "of Pan and the elemental forces, the public has heard a little too much" (*Howards End*, p. 108), he is announcing the end of the late-Victorian tradition in which he himself has participated.[11]

[11] It is impossible here to catalogue the various uses to which mythology was put in late-Victorian literature. Douglas Bush summarizes: "In the latter half of the century there is sufficient evidence that Pan is dead in the almost annual assertions that he is not; and so far as Dionysus could be said to have a renewal of life in the eighties and nineties, the wine of the world was perhaps less potent in nature than when put up in bottles."

Among Forster's three earliest novels, *Where Angels Fear to Tread* is the least saturated with mythological allusions. The values endorsed there—sincerity, spontaneity, and freedom from sexual repression—are "pagan," but the pagan gods do not appear in the novel. There is, to be sure, a trace of Dionysianism embodied in the violence of Gino Carella and symbolized in the "terrible and mysterious" olive trees surrounding Monteriano; and the revelation of Caroline's fruitless desire for Gino strikes Philip as an instance of the "cruel antique malice of the gods." "Centuries of aspiration and culture," Philip thinks, "—and the world could not escape it." (*Where Angels Fear to Tread*, p. 182) Here, at least, Forster is asking us to stand in awe of the force of passion; but it is repression, not passion, whose sway produces the central catastrophe of the novel.[12]

The ambivalence of passion—its potentiality for both destructive and creative results—is equally prominent in *A Room With a View*. The Florentine setting for the early action seems to elicit this duality. "Was there more in her [Florence's] frank beauty than met the eye," asks Forster, "—the power, perhaps, to evoke passions, good and bad, and to bring them speedily to a fulfillment?" (*A Room With a View*, p. 91) Florence witnesses not only the valuable passion of Lucy and George, but also the fatal passion between the two quarrelers in the Piazza Signoria. The blood of the dying man, we remember, spatters Lucy's picture of Venus, showing all too literally the nearness of the two passions of love and wrath. This whole scene is presided over by the pagan gods who inhabit the fountain in the Piazza (pp. 69f.), whose immortality "has come to them after experience, not before. Here, not only in the solitude of Nature, might a hero meet a goddess, or a heroine a god." (pp. 93f.)

(*Mythology and the Romantic Tradition*, p. 396) For the figure of Pan in Forster's novels, see *A Room With a View*, p. 111, and *The Longest Journey*, p. 213.

[12] It is also worth noting that Caroline in her ministrations to the bereaved Gino appears to Philip as a "goddess" (*ibid.*, p. 172), for this is her first moment of instinctive, "pagan" freedom in the novel.

This is plainly a Meredithian gloss on the meeting of George and Lucy. Both Lucy's propriety and George's adolescent *Weltschmerz* must be subdued in the course of the novel, and the process begins here under the aegis of the gods of experience.

Characteristically, Forster reinvokes these early mythological references at later points when the question of passion between George and Lucy is at issue. When she meets him unexpectedly on the Fiesole hillside, Lucy finds George reminiscent of "Heroes—gods—the nonsense of schoolgirls" (p. 116), and when, much later, she has greeted him at the pool near Windy Corner, she reflects that she "had bowed—but to whom? To gods, to heroes, to the nonsense of school-girls! She had bowed across the rubbish that cumbers the world." (pp. 205f.) By recalling his previous words but putting them in a more affirmative context, Forster reveals that Lucy is approaching a conscious knowledge of her true feelings.

This growth of awareness is subtly enhanced by other changes in the novel's pagan allusions. We may remember that the trip to the Fiesole picnic, whose consequences seem at first to be so unpleasant for everyone, is likened to the reckless charioting of Phaethon (see p. 95); while the second kiss, occurring in an English summer rather than an Italian spring, is observed by a sun "guided, not by Phaethon, but by Apollo, competent, unswerving, divine." (p. 226) When George, strengthened by his pagan baptism in the woods, finally succeeds in winning Lucy away from her conventional fears, Lucy has "a sense of deities reconciled." (p. 310) The deities are presumably Aphrodite and Pallas Athene, for Mr. Emerson has just announced, a few lines earlier, that in fighting for love we are also fighting for truth. In accepting George's love Lucy becomes true to her own nature; the familiar Apollonian virtue of self-knowledge emerges side-by-side with passionate love.

Of all Forster's novels, *The Longest Journey* is the most deeply imbued with mythology, and it is also the one whose meaning depends most crucially on our interpretation of its

myths. Its plot, like that of the other two early novels, consists
of a gradual movement away from middle-class prejudice toward
a kind of pagan clear-sightedness, but this movement is complicated by the fact that Rickie Elliot *begins* with a certain
degree of enlightenment. What he must do is to reacquire and
deepen the paganism of his Cambridge days. His pretense that
the elms in his college courtyard are dryads, his personification
of the stars as "gods and heroes," and his frequent retreats to
his private dell near Madingley constitute a pale, literary Hel-
lenism that is nonetheless superior to the "great world" that will
shortly envelop him. The middle section of the book, accordingly, is laden with contrasts between Rickie's mythological
way of apprehending the world and the literal and arid way of
the Pembrokes. These false ascetics have in their hallway a
replica of the Hermes of Praxiteles—"of course only the bust"
(*The Longest Journey*, p. 44), for reasons of decency. The supremely pagan Stephen Wonham indicates the true extent to
which this plaster statuary represents loyalty to Greek values: he
hangs his hat on it and later smashes it to pieces (see pp.
251, 283).

The *gesture* toward paganism, however, is an important feature of the Pembrokes' attitude; their condescending patronage
of mythology expresses the latent flaw in Rickie's own paganism, his lurking belief that the "great world" will invalidate the
truth of the myths. Agnes begins her enticement of Rickie by
faking an interest in dryads, and she momentarily takes the role
of dryad herself (see pp. 88f.); but her true opinion of
Rickie's Greek notion that "poetry, not prose, lies at the core"
is concisely spoken after their marriage: "balder-dash." (p.
201) Rickie will never be capable of the pagan life, but Stephen
and Ansell will at least succeed in rescuing him from the Pembrokes' narrow-sighted conformism.

Mythology is closely interwoven with Rickie's psychological
development. Gerald Dawes, whose bullying he has remembered
in a spirit of masochism, has had the body of a Greek athlete,

and after his death he becomes a kind of god for Rickie. It is Rickie's worship of Gerald, we recall, that lies behind his marriage of Agnes. This becomes relevant when we come across Stephen Wonham, who distinctly resembles Gerald: "the Gerald of history, not the Gerald of romance." (p. 125) Stephen now replaces Gerald as the object of Rickie's devotion; but unlike Gerald, he remains alive to baffle every effort to idolize him. His resemblance to Gerald, in fact, is just sufficient to remind Rickie of his own inadequacy as a surrogate Gerald; for Rickie has, in spite of his intention, gradually "dethroned" Gerald as the consort of his "goddess," Agnes. (p. 80) Stephen's function is thus to draw Rickie out of his symbolic interpretation of things, or rather, to show him that the real symbolic value in his life must be found in relationships deeper than those created by his neurosis. Stephen's "brotherhood" is vital to Rickie, but Stephen will not allow himself to be treated as a brother unless his separate existence is respected; he refuses, for example, to become simply a surrogate for the late Mrs. Elliot. In a sense, therefore, he cautions Rickie against mythology. Though he frees Rickie from the Pembrokes' bondage to society, he also deprives him of his private pantheon and his allegorical daydreams about nature. The Rickie who eventually writes a successful realistic novel has learned, at least temporarily, to take the world at face value.

Forster himself, however, resorts to a good deal of mythology in order to symbolize the issues that Rickie must meet. The most important of his mythological symbols is the figure of Demeter, "the goddess rejoicing in the spring." (p. 289) This is the Demeter whose myth explained the earth, according to Pater, "in its sorrow and its promise, its darkness and its helpfulness to man."[13] She is an embodiment, not just of pastoral gaiety, but of suffering and hope, of disappointment and salvation combined. The photograph of Demeter in Stephen's possession happens to be of a statue that Pater singled out

[13] *Greek Studies*, p. 98.

for special comment. This is the Demeter of Cnidus, discovered in 1857 and transported to the British Museum, where Forster undoubtedly saw it.[14] Pater says of it that it transfixes Demeter "in some pause of her restless wandering over the world in search of the lost child" and that it offers "an abstract type of the wanderer."[15] The description would seem to be relevant to Rickie Elliot's spiritual odyssey in search of his dead mother and lost brother; and Demeter's "shattered knees" in *The Longest Journey* (p. 325, for example), which are a feature of the damaged Cnidian statue, recall the lameness of Rickie, whose own knees are finally shattered by the railroad train that kills him.[16]

The chief function of Forster's Demeter, however, is not to provide a type for the hero but to symbolize a natural principle with which he must come to grips, that of fertility. The elaborate reasoning behind Rickie's decision to marry could be condensed into the statement that he is anxious to make his peace with Demeter. He knows, intellectually, that his home is not in literature or ideality but in the solid physical world, and he wants to recognize his dependence upon nature; yet this nature has made him an orphan and a cripple, and has left him poorly suited for a normal masculine role. Ansell, who is both more practical and more homosexual than Rickie, has no illusions about his own adaptability. When he hears that Rickie is about to become a father he passes by the Cnidian Demeter in the British Museum and thinks to himself frankly "that here were powers he could not cope with, nor, as yet, understand." (p. 210) And Stephen's position is at the opposite pole; being utterly committed to Demeter's spirit, he is the one char-

[14] See his essay, "Cnidus," in *Abinger Harvest*, pp. 173-178.
[15] *Greek Studies*, p. 149.
[16] Rickie's mother may provide a closer parallel to Demeter than Rickie himself. Her spirit searches through the earth for her lost child (Stephen). Her advice to Rickie, to let the Elliots die out, points toward the rebirth in the novel, for Stephen's "springtime" arrives only after Rickie has been killed in rescuing him. These correspondences are of course very approximate and do not suggest the presence of allegory.

acter who can bind himself to future generations of mankind. The pathos of *The Longest Journey* is Rickie's because he alone is capable of self-delusion about his relationship to the natural forces that have produced him.

Submission to Demeter, then, betokens a state of mind nearly opposite to the allegorical consciousness that directs Rickie's and Forster's own short stories. Yet the very employment of Demeter to illustrate this theme is a concession to the old allegorical spirit. Stephen's photograph of Demeter, like Lucy Honeychurch's of Venus, is as blatantly emblematic as the Slough of Despond, and indicates how incompletely *The Longest Journey* answers to its own ideal of art. Still, the more realistic credo is implied, and we are not surprised to find that it has been put into effect in *Howards End*.

Very little is heard of the Greek myths in *Howards End*, and that little is of the nature of burlesque. Leonard Bast's employer, for example, the Porphyrion Corporation, has as its emblem a giant whom Forster likens to an impulsive and obscure Olympian (*Howards End*, p. 139). And the nymphs of modern Hertfordshire, we are told, should properly be depicted as indeterminate, smoky, and insipid, with eyes averted from their approaching urban fate. (see pp. 197f.) Such allusions merely illustrate the author's decision to represent modern life as the unpoetic and specifically un-Greek thing it is.

Howards End is full of symbolism, but it tends to be private and local rather than literary. The obvious symbols to which the story coheres, such as the house, the sword, the inherited library, and the elm tree at Howards End, are drawn from the physical ingredients of the story itself; when the characters seek for meaning they now find it in their immediate experience, not in pictures or books. There is a good deal of emphasis upon pagan legends, but the legends, significantly, are English and are focused directly upon the spot where

Howards End stands.[17] What they signify is essentially what Demeter means in *The Longest Journey*: the characters' involvement with the common lot of humanity, living, dead, and unborn. In *Howards End* this involvement appears not as a threat to "spirituality" but as a saving fact, a refuge from the rootlessness of urbanism and commerce. The insistent theme of "only connect" is served by the attractive power of the local myths, which exert a vague but persistent influence over Ruth Wilcox and Margaret Schlegel. In becoming mistress of the myth-haunted Howards End, Margaret takes a sanctified role as transmitter of the ancient strength and wisdom of her race.

In terms of plot we might say that the cardinal difference between *The Longest Journey* and *Howards End* is that the heroine of the latter novel succeeds, where Rickie fails, in making peace with the prosaic side of her world. Margaret's problem, like Rickie's, is to overcome the fear that no valid meaning is to be found anywhere. She is able to make Forster's demanded "connections" only after she has faced down the goblins of panic and emptiness—mythological figures, if you like—who declare that there is "no such thing as splendour or heroism in the world." (*Howards End*, p. 33) Though she is more adaptable than Rickie, her challenge is also greater: she must preserve her sense of truth and beauty while remaining within the "great world" that Rickie fled. And this new aim would seem to be related to Forster's refinement of technique in drawing the novel's symbolism entirely from the tangible setting of the action. The relative concreteness and self-sufficiency of *Howards End*'s world suggests that Forster has become more willing to take things as they are found. He, too, sees the folly of turning one's back on the Wilcoxes, and his achievement in making them believable (compare, for instance, Henry Wilcox with Herbert Pembroke for "roundness" of character) undoubtedly owes much to this more resigned and realistic attitude.

[17] Note, e.g., the refrain of allusions to the wych-elm at Howards End that has a vaguely druidic tradition attached to it. *ibid.*, pp. 3, 22, 71f., 189f., 206.

In *A Passage to India*, finally, the mythology of harmony with the earth is inconspicuous, for the good reason that harmony with the Indian earth means madness. Indeed, the pervasive theme of the irreconcilability of the human order with the divine or natural is destructive of the very idea of humanistic symbolism. Yet *A Passage to India* is an intricately symbolic novel, in which the slightest details of landscape or plot can carry hints of transcendental secrets. The dominant symbol of the Marabar Caves and their echoes strikes a note of anti-meaning that reverberates throughout the book. No extraneous myths need intrude to underline the humanistic moral, for the moral itself disappears in the face of a paralyzing vision of disorder.

We shall find that the quest for meaning that was partially rewarded in the lives of Philip Herriton and Caroline Abbott, of Lucy Honeychurch and George Emerson, of Rickie Elliot, and of Margaret Schlegel, becomes futile and even ridiculous in *A Passage to India*. Aziz, who "desired to remember his wife and could not" (*A Passage to India*, p. 56); Adela Quested, who thinks that the pressure of Ronny Heaslop's hand "surely meant something" (p. 94), but discovers the contrary; Cyril Fielding, whose moment of possible enlightenment passes by "with averted face and on swift wings" (p. 191); and Mrs. Moore, who is incapable of entertaining "one large thought" (p. 208) after her mystical realization that all value resolves itself to "boum"—all these characters are victims of Forster's intensified doubts about the usefulness of that undignified organ, the human mind. The process we have traced in Forster's art, of increasing deference to the hostile or indifferent powers by whose leave we exist, is here carried one step too far. The humanistic virtue of looking steadily at the world develops into a compulsion to gaze helplessly into the abyss.

In the contrast between the inhibited English colonials and several unselfconscious, sexually vigorous, and "godlike" Indians, however, there are echoes of Forster's earlier mythological devices. The most striking of these references occurs in the court-room scene, when Adela Quested, who is trying to recall whether Aziz wanted to rape her or vice versa, notices an Indian menial who is operating the fan: "Almost naked, and splendidly formed . . . he caught her attention as she came in, and he seemed to control the proceedings. He had the strength and beauty that sometimes come to flower in Indians of low birth. When that strange race nears the dust and is condemned as untouchable, then nature remembers the physical perfection that she accomplished elsewhere, and throws out a god—not many, but one here and there, to prove to society how little its categories impress her. . . . Pulling the rope towards him, relaxing it rhythmically, sending swirls of air over others, receiving none himself, he seemed apart from human destinies, a male fate, a winnower of souls." (p. 217)

The physique of this man (to say nothing of his portentous movements) possibly helps Adela to recall the attraction she felt for Aziz, his countryman, for she withdraws her charges shortly afterward. His mythical power is nothing more or less than his sexuality, but it is more effective in every sense than Forster's earlier allusions to Venus and Demeter.

There are, to be sure, "thematic" literary allusions in A Passage to India, but they refer to the literature of Islam and Hinduism, and are unobtrusively woven into Forster's narrative of events. No longer are the characters required to trudge around with photographs of their patron gods and goddesses, and no longer do they speak in mottoes quoted or paraphrased from Shelley, Butler, and Meredith. These are unnecessary because Forster's intent is now metaphysical, not moral. Instead of recommending that we behave in such-and-such a way, his novel tries simply to show us an image of our drastic plight as human beings.

This progress in Forster's career may be understood if we borrow (and abuse) the Nietzschean terms with which we began. Forster's tone in A Passage to India is more "Apollonian" than ever in its sober dismissal of romantic illusions, yet this is also the most poetic of his novels, in the sense that poetry seeks for images to state the felt relationship between man and his universe. To show the relative insignificance of morality against a background of total disorder is to have given the Dionysian principle its due. Here Forster turns over his art, for the first and apparently the last time, to a single controlling vision, which, though it eclipses his humanism, finally produces a novel with something of the power and wholeness of a myth itself. Such an art, in Nietzsche's words, "may transform these horrible reflections on the terror and absurdity of existence into representations with which man may live."[18]

[18] *The Birth of Tragedy. The Philosophy of Nietzsche*, p. 985.

Ten

A PASSAGE TO INDIA

A *Passage to India* (1924), deservedly the best-known of Forster's novels, is also the most difficult to interpret consistently. Critics have generally recognized that, philosophically, it is Forster's most ambitious work, but not everyone has professed to be happy with this fact; the novel's story, we are sometimes told, is too frail to bear the weight of its supposed metaphysical implications. Furthermore, what are those implications, and how do they bear upon the narrower issues of ethics and Empire that are raised? The novel has inspired some perceptive critics to reach quite opposite conclusions as to its ethical point of view. It seems to me, however, that Lionel Trilling comes closest to the truth when he says that A *Passage to India*, rather than telling us what is to be done, simply restates the familiar political and social dilemmas in the light of the total human situation.[1]

Such a light, of course, must be cast from a great distance; hence the necessity for extreme detachment in the tone of Forster's narrative and commentary. Hence, too, the incongruity between the novel's trivial action and its hints of enormous meaning. This incongruity is essential to Forster's intentions; indeed, if I were to assign a single theme to A *Passage to India*, I would call it the incongruity between aspiration and reality. Religiously, politically, and simply in terms of the characters' efforts to get along with one another, this incongruity is pervasive. The strands of the novel are unified by the thematic principle that unity is not to be obtained, and the plot is trivial because Forster's restatements of the ordinary questions imply

[1] E. M. *Forster*, p. 138.

that all of human life, whether great or small in our customary opinion, is ensnared in pettiness.

It may be difficult at first to adjust our critical focus to this lofty contemplation of man's helplessness, yet the departure from Forster's earlier novels is not extreme. Even in *Where Angels Fear to Tread*, we remember, Philip Herriton's conclusion is that life is greater but less complete than he has supposed; he discovers that his humanistic virtues have not really led him to an understanding of the world. *A Room With a View*, though it ends pleasantly enough for its heroine, suggests, in the Carlylean agnosticism of the Emersons, a similar uneasiness about the ultimate order. In *The Longest Journey* all three of the central male characters suspect that the universe is indifferent or hostile to humanity. And the satisfactory conclusion to *Howards End* is reached, not by Margaret Schlegel's having acquiesced in the providential scheme, but through her striving against the panic and emptiness of a godless world. In each of the four novels there *is* a measure of heroism, but it is always strictly bordered by a sense of human limitation. The difference in emphasis between these books and *A Passage to India* is simply that the latter neglects to overcome the latent fear of chaos; it continues to illustrate the humanistic struggle against meaninglessness, but fails to affirm that a victory is possible.

The situation of the novel is partly familiar, partly new. In several ways the basic contrast between India and England, or between India and Anglo-India, brings us back to the world of *Where Angels Fear to Tread* and *A Room with a View*. The English sexual prudery, the emphasis on duty and good form, the distrust of everything foreign are all brought into expected relief against the spontaneity of a manifestly un-English country. The colonial administrators of Chandrapore and their bigoted wives stumble through a typically comic series of misinterpretations of India and individual Indians, just as the earlier tourists misinterpret Italy; and some of the central English characters—Adela Quested, Cyril Fielding, Mrs. Moore—un-

dergo the customary Forsterian shift of sympathy toward the
"native" point of view. Socially, however, the novel is much
more complicated than the earlier ones. India, too, has a strati-
fied society, one that is in fact more rigidly discriminatory than
England's; and the Indian protagonist, Aziz, is only slightly
closer to, say, Gino Carella than are the Englishmen in the
novel. He, too, is restrained on all sides by barriers of class and
race.

Similarly, we look in vain for romantic suggestions that India,
like Italy, stands for a passionate release of the human spirit;
India is apparently more of a muddle than a mystery, and it
distinctly does not embody a tidy moral for the English visitors
to ponder on their way home. This brings us to a basic difference
in the way Forster now regards his subject-matter. The foreign
civilization is no longer a moralized backdrop to the novel's
action, but is itself a kind of protagonist. It is not simply that
we come to know the Indian Aziz more thoroughly than any of
the English characters, but that the image of India as a whole
is more important than any of the figures, English or Indian,
who move across it. To understand India is to understand the
rationale of the whole creation; but the characters do not understand it, and Forster's plot makes us ask whether human faculties are capable of such understanding at all. After each character has made his feeble effort to grasp the total pattern, we are
left again with the enormous and irrational presence of India,
a riddle that can be ignored but never solved.

The literal plot of *A Passage to India* seems at first to be un-
related to this symbolic level of meaning. Its chief issue is one
that is suitable to a detective story: whether or not Aziz has actually attempted to rape Adela Quested in the Marabar Caves.
This, however, is bound up with the whole problem of Anglo-
Indian misunderstanding, for the occasion of the supposed assault is a picnic organized by Aziz in the interest of interracial
friendship. Adela's near-disastrous hallucination is, completely
apart from its religious implications, a symbolic breakdown of

the effort at mutual sympathy between the two countries. Adela herself has come to Chandrapore not simply to marry Ronny Heaslop, the City Magistrate, but to "know India" on its own terms. Mrs. Moore, too, her traveling-companion and Ronny's mother, has come with a willingness to understand and love the Indians. Much of the early by-play of the plot is taken up with the efforts of Adela and Mrs. Moore to be generous toward India—efforts that are thwarted not by Indians, but by the suspicious and snobbish colonial officials, including Ronny Heaslop. When a genuine rapport between East and West seems finally imminent, however, it is shown to be impossible. Indians and Englishmen must remain apart, not because Indians are venal and shifty (as Ronny and his friends believe) but because of fundamental differences in temperament, social structure, and religious outlook. The one hope for unity is, as we might expect, a trust in the power of affectionate friendship among individuals; but even this proves inadequate, as we find in the crumbling of relations between Aziz and Cyril Fielding, the liberal and humane principal of Chandrapore's Government College.

A *Passage to India*, then, finally refuses all bids for "passage" through the national barriers it defines; the more earnest the gestures of personal good will, the more thoroughly they are resented and misconstrued on both sides. Such a novel can have no hero or villain, since the blame for the failure of communication rests on the whole conflict of civilizations, indeed upon human nature generally. Because this is so, the novel dwells less upon single personalities than its four predecessors; instead of following one character's internal debate between values represented by a few other characters, we stand before a social panorama in which a multitude of "flat" characters are briefly glimpsed.

Thus, on the English side, we shift our main focus continually among Adela, Mrs. Moore, and Fielding, none of whom matches the complexity of Rickie Elliot or Margaret Schlegel; and after these, and perhaps Ronny, we become briefly acquainted with a series of insignificant persons whose natures can be summed up in a phrase. There is Major Callendar, the Civil Surgeon, who is rude to Aziz but knows that Aziz is professionally superior to him; Mr. Turton, the well-meaning but jingoistic Collector; his wife, who speaks Urdu but knows only the imperative mood; Miss Derek, a prankster chiefly memorable for her expletives ("golly!" "how putrid!" and so on); the Reverends Graysford and Sorley, timid missionaries; Mr. McBryde, the District Superintendent of Police, whom Forster calls the most reflective and best educated of the Chandrapore officials, but who firmly maintains that all persons born south of latitude thirty are criminals at heart; and several others, some of whom appear only for a sentence or a paragraph.

Among the Indians, Aziz and the Hindu Professor Godbole are important and are sharply portrayed, but behind them stand rows of characters whose nearly unanimous contempt for the English tends to blur their individuality. There is the Nawab Bahadur, who argues against superstition but believes in ghosts; Mahmoud Ali, Aziz's genially cynical friend who hates the British but loves the memory of Queen Victoria; Mohammed Latif, "a gentle, happy and dishonest old man" (p. 14) who humbly but doggedly poaches on his distant relations; Hamidullah, a Cambridge graduate who wistfully deplores the "wire-pulling and fear" of Chandrapore's political atmosphere (see p. 107); Aziz's servant Hassan, an accomplished shirker; Dr. Panna Lal, whose low social position licenses Aziz to make an enemy of him; the magistrate Das, who tries unsuccessfully to befriend Aziz after presiding over the trial; and numerous other figures of incidental importance. Forster underscores the profusion of levels to Indian society. We are told, for example, that in addition to the miserable clients who wait in the dust outside Chandrapore's courthouse, "there were circles even beyond these —people who wore nothing but a loincloth, people who wore not even that, and spent their lives in knocking two sticks together before a scarlet doll—humanity grading and drifting beyond the educated vision, until no earthly invitation can embrace it." (p. 37)

Sentences like this last one suggest more than they directly say; they lead us to search for some controlling view of life behind the observed fact that is reported. In this case Forster has used two related metaphors that are picked up and elaborated elsewhere with metaphysical overtones. These are the metaphors of *receding circles* and of *invitation*. In A *Passage to India* Forster habitually allows his vision to slide outward from a human "circle" of perspective to a macrocosmic one, so that we come to see the lives of his characters as a tiny, though possibly central, spot in the total pattern. The very first chapter, which resembles that of *Nostromo* in its portentous fixing of the scale of action, makes striking use of this device. At night over Chandrapore, "the stars hang like lamps from the immense vault. The distance between the vault and them is as nothing to the distance behind them, and that farther distance, though beyond colour, last freed itself from blue." (p. 9) Forster's syntax here is confusing, but his meaning is sufficiently clear: the scale of measurement suggested by the part of the universe visible to man is insignificantly small compared with the colorless (and hence valueless) realm beyond it.

Later in the novel Forster is more insistent about this dwarfing of humanity. Thus while a group of Englishmen are speaking together at a garden party, "their words seemed to die as soon as uttered. Some kites hovered overhead, impartial, over the kites passed the mass of a vulture, and with an impartiality exceeding all, the sky, not deeply coloured but translucent, poured light from its whole circumference. It seemed unlikely that the series stopped here. Beyond the sky must not there be something that overarches all the skies, more impartial even than they? Beyond which again. . . ." (pp. 39f.) Here the importance of man is qualified not only by the predatory kites and vulture, suggesting death, but more horribly by the concentric spheres of "impartiality," that is, of divine indifference to the human world. Mrs. Moore, the Christian, begins to doubt whether the name of Jehovah can be meaningful in the vast impersonality of India. "Outside the arch there seemed always an arch," she reflects, "beyond the remotest echo a silence." (p. 52)

Another disquieting feature of India is the constant surrounding presence of the jungle. Unlike England, whose modest proportions and mild climate encourage the illusion of harmony between man and nature (Ronny and Adela, significantly, have had "serious walks and talks" at Grasmere), India is frankly unimpressed by man. "Bats, rats, birds, insects will as soon nest inside a house as out; it is to them a normal growth of the eternal jungle, which alternately produces houses trees, houses trees." (p. 35) The animals of England are scarcely more considerate, of course, "but in the tropics the indifference is more prominent, the inarticulate world is closer at hand and readier to resume control as soon as men are tired." (p. 114)

It is in these conditions that Forster develops his metaphor of invitation. The offering or withholding of invitations, which is the Englishman's characteristic means of keeping his life in proper social order, becomes ineffectual when such "guests" as tigers and cobras may drop in at any time. And this fact presents a challenge to the whole Western Christian mind, as we can see in the following passage:

"All invitations must proceed from heaven perhaps; perhaps it is futile for men to initiate their own unity, they do but widen the gulfs between them by the attempt. So at all events thought old Mr. Graysford and young Mr. Sorley. . . . In our Father's house are many mansions, they taught, and there alone will the incompatible multitudes of mankind be welcomed and soothed. Not one shall be turned away by the servants on that verandah, be he black or white, not one shall be kept standing who approaches with a loving heart. And why should the divine hospitality cease here? Consider, with all reverence, the monkeys. May there not be a mansion for the monkeys also? Old Mr. Graysford said No, but young Mr. Sorley, who was advanced, said Yes; he saw no reason why monkeys should not have their collateral share of bliss, and he had sympathetic discussions about them with his Hindu friends. And the jackals? Jackals were indeed less to Mr. Sorley's mind, but he admitted that the mercy of God, being infinite, may well embrace all mammals. And the wasps? He became uneasy during the descent to wasps, and was apt to change the conversation. And oranges, cactuses, crystals and mud? and the bacteria inside Mr. Sorley? No, no, this is going too far. We must exclude someone from our gathering, or we shall be left with nothing." (pp. 37f.)

Forster is of course being deliberately absurd in pressing the social metaphor to these lengths. He is implying, with logical irony, that Christianity cannot afford to slacken its "inhospitality" to chaos; as soon as one opens the doors of heaven a crack wider, the whole idea of bodily resurrection is invaded with contradictions. Human kind, as a Christian poet has put it, cannot bear very much reality.

On one level the idea of invitation is perfectly literal in *A Passage to India*; the social tangle of the novel is adumbrated in the repeated question of whether Englishmen and Indians should entertain one another. Early in the novel, under pressure from Adela and Mrs. Moore, the English colonials agree to include Indians in a bridge party, but their continuing suspicion and snobbery prevent any real mingling of the races; the occasion becomes an embarrassing image of apartheid. Again, Aziz's invitation to Adela, Mrs. Moore, and Fielding to inspect the Marabar Caves is an ill-starred gesture of friendliness. Even Fielding's private entertainment of Aziz with the two ladies ends in misunderstanding; Ronny, who has the Forsterian egoist's gift of believing precisely the opposite of what is true, arrives on the scene and suggests to Fielding that Aziz cannot be trusted with the delectable Miss Quested. The Indians themselves are divided along religious lines and are no closer to unity at the end of the novel than at the beginning. The flurry of camaraderie following the trial is quickly replaced by the ancient distrust between

Moslem and Hindu, while the breach between Indians and English is wider than ever. Fielding, the one character who has temporarily "belonged" to both sides, understands the futility of his liberalism and departs from India altogether. The very spirit of the Indian earth, Forster says, "tries to keep men in compartments" (p. 127), and in the final sentence of the novel the sky and earth together are pictured as conspiring against mutual understanding.

On another level of interpretation, this social impasse opens out into the religious question that the Reverends Graysford and Sorley handle so gingerly: whether God's attention extends to all His creatures, to some of them, or to none. It is significant, for instance, that the famous image of the wasp in *A Passage to India* is introduced just after Ronny has tried to discourage his mother from associating with Aziz, and just before Aziz is invited to the bridge party by Mr. Turton. Mrs. Moore finds a wasp on a coat-peg and, in calling it "Pretty dear" (p. 35), acknowledges its right to existence; she "invites" it into the circle of her benevolent interest. The Reverend Sorley, however, draws the line precisely at wasps; he must concede that it is really too much to ask that God should bother with them. Much later in the novel the figure of the wasp is introduced in the mind of Professor Godbole, who remembers Mrs. Moore and a wasp with the same spiritual tenderness: "He loved the wasp equally, he impelled it likewise, he was imitating God." (p. 286) The Westerners and Moslems in *A Passage to India*, considering themselves distinct from God and from one another, are inhospitable to insects, and the enmity seems mutual. Aziz is repeatedly upset by the presence of flies in his house, and Fielding, the Western rationalist, is pursued by bees. (pp. 102, 279, 299) Mrs. Moore and Professor Godbole extend their love to wasps because their religions—his is Hinduism, hers a sporadic mysticism overlaying her Christian training—accept the entire creation as an indivisible part of God's being.

Is the novel, then, a covert apology for Hinduism? Many readers have thought so, but at the expense of oversimplifying Forster's attitude. Hinduism is certainly the religion most able to cope with the bewildering contradictions one finds in India, but its method of doing this—accepting everything indiscriminately, obliterating all distinctions—has obvious disadvantages that are brought out in the course of the novel. The tripartite structure of *A Passage to India*, with its formal shifting from "Mosque" to "Caves" to "Temple," suggests that various religious paths to truth are being problematically offered; and the inconclusive and frustrating ending of the book implies that each path, while having particular advantages that the others lack, ultimately ends in a maze.

Those who favor a Hindu reading of *A Passage to India* rest their claims on the final section of the novel, where the setting has changed from Westernized Chandrapore to a Hindu Native State. In these surroundings there is, indeed, occasion for a meeting of East and West. But the meeting, which takes place at the peak of the Hindu festival of Gokul Ashtami, is effected through the capsizing of two boats in a furious rainstorm, and it is a moot question whether the momentarily reconciled parties have been drenched with Hindu love or simply drenched. It is a climax, Forster warns, only "as far as India admits of one" (p. 315), and in retrospect the festival amounts only to "ragged edges of religion . . . unsatisfactory and undramatic tangles." (p. 316) If Hinduism succeeds, where Islam and Christianity fail, in taking the entire universe into its view, we still cannot silence the voice of Western humanism. What about man and his need for order? Are we to sacrifice our notion of selfhood to the ideal of inclusiveness? "The fact is," Forster has said elsewhere, "we can only love what we know personally." (*Two Cheers*, p. 45) And as Fielding thinks when he has quit India and recovered his sense of proportion at Venice, "Without form, how can there be beauty?" (p. 282)

These misgivings about reading A *Passage to India* in a spirit of orthodoxy are strengthened by an acquaintance with Forster's private statements of opinion about the religions involved. We know, of course, that such statements cannot take the place of internal evidence, but in this case the internal evidence is somewhat ambiguous; the temptation to ask Forster what he really thinks is irresistible. His attitude toward Christianity is hardly obscure, but Islam and Hinduism have aroused mixed feelings in him, and these, I think, find their way into A *Passage to India*. On his second trip to India, in 1921, Forster was Private Secretary to the Maharajah of Dewas State Senior, a Hindu Native State; his letters from there and elsewhere are sometimes revealing. "I do like Islam," he wrote to his mother from Chhatarpur, "though I have had to come through Hinduism to discover it. After all the mess and profusion and confusion of Gokul Ashtami, where nothing ever stopped or need ever have begun, it was like standing on a mountain."[2]

The nature of this attraction is evident in two essays reprinted in *Abinger Harvest*, "Salute to the Orient!" and "The Mosque." Islamic meditation, Forster explains, "though it has the intensity and aloofness of mysticism, never leads to abandonment of personality. The Self is precious, because God, who created it, is Himself a personality. . . ." (*Abinger Harvest*, p. 273) One thinks immediately of Forster's well-known individualism; the idea of selfhood is indispensable to his entire system of value. Again, Forster's liberalism and his contempt for superstition seem to govern the following contrasts between Islam and Christianity: "Equality before God—so doubtfully proclaimed by Christianity—lies at the very root of Islam . . ." and the Moslem God "was never incarnate and left no cradles, coats, handkerchiefs or nails on earth to stimulate and complicate devotion." (*Ibid.*, pp. 275, 276) Nowhere does Forster imply that he actually believes the dogmatic content of Islam; the point is that he is aesthetically gratified by a religion that is not

[2] *The Hill of Devi* (New York, 1953), p. 193.

grossly anthropomorphic. He is no more of a Moslem than he is a Christian, but Islam at least does not outrage his common sense and his love of modest form.

A Passage to India, of course, demands more of religion than this; the central question of the novel is that of man's relationship to God, and Moslems, Forster says, "do not seek to be God or even to see Him." (*Ibid.*, p. 273) Thus Islam can hardly lead Forster's characters to the assurance they need; as Fielding puts it, " 'There is no God but God' doesn't carry us far through the complexities of matter and spirit; it is only a game with words, really, a religious pun, not a religious truth." (*A Passage to India*, p. 276) And the refusal to abandon personality, which is the strongest bond between Aziz and the Westerners in the novel, turns out to be a severe limitation in their apparatus for grasping transcendent truth.

Forster's opinion of Hinduism is more clearly a dual one: he finds Hindu ritual absurd but Hindu theology relatively attractive. His letters about Gokul Ashtami are extremely condescending; he thought the spirit of the festival indistinguishable from "ordinary mundane intoxication," and he generalized: "What troubles me is that every detail, almost without exception, is fatuous and in bad taste."[3] Yet his admiration for the Maharajah for whom he was later to work led him to an early sympathy with Hindu doctrine. The following excerpt from a letter of March 6, 1913 explains part of the Maharajah's position and Forster's response to it:

"His attitude was very difficult for a Westerner. He believes that we—men, birds, everything—are part of God, and that men have developed more than birds because they have come nearer to realising this.

"That isn't so difficult; but when I asked why we had any of us ever been severed from God, he explained it by God becoming unconscious that we were parts of him, owing to his energy at some time being concentrated elsewhere. . . . Salvation,

[3] *The Hill of Devi*, pp. 160, 159.

then, is the thrill we feel when God again becomes conscious of us, and all our life we must train our perceptions so that we may be capable of feeling when the time comes.

"I think I see what lies at the back of this—if you believe that the universe was God's *conscious* creation, you are faced with the fact that he has consciously created suffering and sin, and this the Indian refuses to believe. 'We were either put here intentionally or unintentionally,' said the Rajah, 'and it raises fewer difficulties if we suppose that it was unintentionally.' "[4]

Here again we may observe that Forster is not asserting a religious belief of his own, but is simply trying to be open-minded. Still, we can recognize the congeniality of Hinduism, in this interpretation, to Forster's opinions as we already know them. His disbelief in Providence, his sense of man's ignorance of divine truth, his rejection of the idea of a man-centered universe—all are reconcilable with his summary of the Maharajah's Hinduism. Yet the point at which the correspondence breaks down is even more striking. It is easy enough for Forster to entertain the theory that God is presently unconscious of man, but there is little provision in his philosophy for the moment of awakening; only the negative side of Hinduism accords with his temperament.

There is no escaping the impression that Hinduism is treated with considerable sympathy in *A Passage to India*. Its chief function, however, seems to be to discredit the Christian and Moslem emphasis on personality; the vastness and confusion of India are unsuitable for an orderly, benevolent deity whose attention to individuals is tireless. When the question of mystical union arises, however, Forster becomes evasive in the extreme. Gokul Ashtami, he remarks, presents "emblems of passage; a passage not easy, not now, not here, not to be apprehended except when it is unattainable. . . ." (A *Passage to India*, pp. 314f.) Although Hinduism offers the most engaging fable to describe our isolation from meaning, it, too, like Islam and

[4] *ibid.*, p. 45.

Christianity, seems powerless before the nihilistic message of the Marabar Caves.

The incidents in the Caves are of course the symbolic heart of the novel, where India exerts its force of illusion and disillusion upon the British visitors. These incidents are meaningful on all levels, making the hopeless misunderstanding between East and West vivid and complete, but their most important kind of meaning is clearly religious. The Christian Mrs. Moore and the Moslem Aziz, having befriended one another in a mosque, have previously been kept apart by social barriers, but now they are to meet, with Adela, on the ground of what Adela has called "the real India." The Marabar Caves will offer them an India more virginal than they bargain for, and will, through utter indifference to selfhood, challenge their very sense of reality.

The Marabar Hills, "older than all spirit," date back to an age long before Hinduism arrived and "scratched and plastered a few rocks." (p. 124) They are "flesh of the sun's flesh," and the sun "may still discern in their outline forms that were his before our globe was torn from his bosom." (p. 123) They are thus completely divorced from the works and history of man. Like the Hindu God, they seem to have no attributes: "Nothing, nothing attaches to them," says Forster. (p. 124) And this analogy with Hinduism is highly suggestive, for Mrs. Moore's experience in the Hills is a kind of parody of the recognition of Brahma. Hinduism claims that Self and Not-self, Atman and Brahman, are actually one, and that the highest experience is to perceive this annihilation of value. Value is indeed annihilated for Mrs. Moore; the echoing Caves convince her that "Everything exists, nothing has value." (p. 149)

Glen O. Allen has found several references in the *Upanishads* to the dwelling of Atman and Brahman in caves,[5] and one such passage seems especially pertinent here. "The wise who, by

[5] Glen O. Allen, "Structure, Symbol, and Theme in E. M. Forster's *A Passage to India*," PMLA, lxx (December 1955), 934-954.

means of meditation on his Self, recognises the Ancient, who is difficult to be seen, who has entered into the dark, who is hidden in the cave, who dwells in the abyss, as God, he indeed leaves joy and sorrow far behind."[6] In the Marabar Caves Mrs. Moore discovers "the ancient," but it is not Brahma: "What had spoken to her in that scoured-out cavity of the granite? What dwelt in the first of the caves? Something very old and very small. Before time, it was before space also. Something snub-nosed, incapable of generosity—the undying worm itself." (p. 208) And though she does, indeed, leave joy and sorrow behind, the departure is utterly pedestrian. She has simply been thrust into the disillusion of old age: "She had come to that state where the horror of the universe and its smallness are both visible at the same time—the twilight of the double vision in which so many elderly people are involved. If this world is not to our taste, well, at all events there is Heaven, Hell, Annihilation—one or other of those large things, that huge scenic background of stars, fires, blue or black air. All heroic endeavor, and all that is known as art, assumes that there is such a background . . . But in the twilight of the double vision, a spiritual muddledom is set up for which no high-sounding words can be found; we can neither act nor refrain from action, we can neither ignore nor respect Infinity." (pp. 207f.)

Readers who have claimed that Mrs. Moore has suddenly been transformed from a modest Christian to a mystical Brahmin have had to overlook the prosaic quality of her feelings here. She has had, in effect, an antivision, a realization that to see through the world of superficial appearances is to be left with nothing at all. "The abyss also may be petty, the serpent of eternity made of maggots. . . ." (p. 208)

Mrs. Moore's inversion of Hinduism is sharpened by the resemblance of the Caves' echoes—"boum" and "ou-boum"—to the mystic Hindu syllable "Om," which stands for the trinity of

[6] *The Sacred Books of the East*, ed. F. Max Müller (Oxford, 1884), Vol. xv: *The Upanishads*, p. 10.

the godhead. He who ponders this syllable, says the *Prasna-Upanishad*, "learns to see the all-pervading, the Highest Person."[7] This is Mrs. Moore's ambition: "To be one with the universe! So dignified and simple." (p. 208) In an ironical sense she achieves this, for she does grasp a oneness underlying everything. Its monotony, however, is subversive of the moral and ceremonial distinctions that we require to reconcile ourselves to the Absolute. ". . . Religion appeared, poor little talkative Christianity, and she knew that all its divine words from 'Let there be Light' to 'It is finished' only amounted to 'boum.'" (p. 150) The oneness Mrs. Moore has found has obliterated her belief in the categories of space and time, distinctions that are essential to a religion whose God has a sense of history. This is why she can be said to have perceived both the horror and the smallness of the universe; the Marabar Caves "robbed infinity and eternity of their vastness, the only quality that accommodates them to mankind." (p. 150)

If I may digress for a moment, this debasement of the ideas of infinity and eternity seems to be philosophically suggestive. The modern Western sense of time, which was once thought to correspond exactly and immutably with the objective world, and which kept its "universality" even after Kant proved it to be subjective, has been challenged from various sides by physicists, anthropologists, and psychoanalysts. Norman O. Brown, in summarizing the arguments that time is culturally relative, says that the progressive and irreversible time of the Newtonian universe is, in effect, a legacy of religion; it is geared to a day of redemption at the end of "history." Archaic religion, with its annual atonements, is "cyclical, periodic, unhistoric." And at a still more primitive level we meet Freud's great discovery that the unconscious mind observes no time schema at all. Our time-sense, if Brown is correct, is ultimately ruled by repression —by the effort to manage and spend a primordial unconscious feeling of guilt. In these terms it seems highly appropriate that

[7] Quoted by Allen, *PMLA*, LXX, 943.

both Mrs. Moore and Adela (see below, p. 161) find their sense of time disrupted in the "prehistoric" Caves. Both women are gripped by previously unconscious feelings which their religion customarily placates or denies; in both cases Forster strikes an oblique blow at Christianity by implying that its time-sense is dependent on repression.[8]

We may well ask at this point why Mrs. Moore, who seems to have a kind of second sight on occasion and who is certainly a morally sympathetic character, is visited with disillusionment. One answer may simply be that she *does* have second sight, that she perceives what truly subsists behind the veil of Maya; in this case her experience would constitute a thorough disavowal of Hinduism on Forster's part. Remembering Adela's hallucination, however, we may question whether Mrs. Moore has penetrated anything at all. Perhaps she has merely heard echoes of her own unvoiced misgivings about the significance of life.[9] It is impossible, in any case, to support the popular reading that she has experienced the merging of Atman and Brahman. Atman is the presence of the *universal* ego in the individual, the "God dwelling within," and the properly disciplined Hindu will find Brahman, the supreme soul, echoed in this "Self." Mrs. Moore, however, is unprepared to relinquish her selfhood in the narrow sense of personality. Instead of blending her identity with that

[8] See Norman O. Brown, *Life Against Death; The Psychoanalytical Meaning of History* (New York, 1959), pp. 273-278. If Brown is right in treating the Newtonian sense of reality as a stepchild of religion, Forster also seems vindicated in his treatment of the rationalist, Fielding. Fielding has little to offer in the ontological debate of the novel, for his religious outlook is simply the Christian one minus God and the Savior. Though Fielding and Adela seem dissimilar, they are philosophically quite close, and it is proper that they should recognize their common impasse in trying to "understand India" (see below, pp. 161ff.).

[9] The Caves not only deliver a dull echo in reply to every sound, they also offer reflections of light on their polished walls. The flame of a match and its reflection, we are told, "approach and strive to unite, but cannot, because one of them breathes air, the other stone." (p. 125) In symbolic terms this seems to support the idea that one will "see" his own thoughts imprisoned in Marabar stone, i.e. robbed of their context of human illusion.

of the world-soul, she reduces the world-soul to the scale of her own wearied ego; her dilettantish yearning for oneness with the universe has been echoed, not answered. Whether or not Forster considers the serpent of eternity to be made of maggots is a question we cannot answer on the basis of A *Passage to India*; in view of his skepticism it is doubtful that he would feel himself qualified to make any assertion at all on the subject. What does emerge clearly from the novel is that the Marabar Caves have not brought us into the presence of ultimate truth. The last words of India to Mrs. Moore, as she sails away to die, may serve also as a caveat to eager critics: "So you thought an echo was India; you took the Marabar caves as final? . . . What have we in common with them, or they with Asirgarh? Good-bye!" (p. 210)

Adela's experience in the Cave, though it has religious implications, lends itself more readily to analysis in psychological terms. This agrees with the Caves' function of echoing only what is brought to them, for Adela's yearnings are sexual, not mystical. As she climbs upward with Aziz her conscious thoughts are occupied with her approaching marriage to Ronny, but she is increasingly troubled by misgivings, until she realizes with vexation that she is not in love with her fiancé. Before entering the Cave, however, she commits the Forsterian heresy of deciding that love is not essential to a successful marriage; she will marry Ronny anyway. As in the case of Mrs. Moore, the Marabar Caves thrust to the surface a conflict between conventional and suppressed feelings. The echo that is metaphorically sounded in Adela's hallucination (if it is a hallucination) of sexual attack is that of her unvoiced desire for physical love.

That this problematic assault should be attributed to Aziz is perhaps the central irony of plot in A *Passage to India*. Forster takes pains to let us know that Aziz's thoughts about sex are "hard and direct, though not brutal" (p. 102)—exactly the reverse of Adela's. Though he generally "upheld the proprieties . . . he did not invest them with any moral halo, and it was here that he chiefly differed from an Englishman." (p. 103) As for Adela, he finds her sexually repellent ("She has practically no breasts," he tells Fielding; p. 120), whereas Adela, for her part, is attracted to him ("What a handsome little Oriental he was . . ."; p. 152). Just before she enters the Cave, whose significance is apparently Freudian as well as metaphysical, Adela enviously ponders Aziz's physical advantages: "beauty, thick hair, a fine skin." (p. 153) She asks him, in what Forster calls "her honest, decent, inquisitive way: 'Have you one wife or more than one?'" (p. 153) And when the monogamous widower Aziz passes into a Cave to hide his embarrassment over her question, Adela enters a different Cave, "thinking with half her mind 'sight-seeing bores me,' and wondering with the other half about marriage." (p. 153) It is this other half, this wondering about physical gratification, that accosts her in the Cave; and, since Self and Not-self are confused there, she assigns her thoughts to Aziz.

An important difference between Adela's crisis and Mrs. Moore's is that Mrs. Moore adjusts her whole view of life to accord with the annihilation of value in the Cave, while Adela continues for a while to be torn between accepting and rejecting her experience. Mrs. Moore knows intuitively that Aziz is not a rapist, but she is weary of legalistic distinctions; the alleged crime "presented itself to her as love: in a cave, in a church—Boum, it amounts to the same." (p. 208) She does not stay to testify for Aziz, for the moral issue of the trial cannot interest her; if there is no value in the universe, there is surely none in distinctions between sanctioned and illicit love. Yet this very indifference makes it proper that Mrs. Moore, after she has withered out of bodily existence, should be resurrected as a Hindu goddess in the minds of the Indians at Aziz's trial. "When all the ties of the heart are severed here on earth," says the *Katha-Upanishad*, "then the mortal becomes immortal. . . ."[10] The parallel is in one sense ironic, as we have seen: Mrs. Moore

[10] *The Sacred Books of the East*, xv, 23.

has been the victim of a travesty of Hindu enlightenment. On the other hand, the Mrs. Moore who originally befriended Aziz and who is remembered fondly by Professor Godbole has believed in loving everything that enters her consciousness, and such a love is the cornerstone of Hinduism.

Unlike Mrs. Moore, Adela lacks the imagination to be permanently shattered by her irrational experience. "In space things touch, in time things part" (p. 193), she repeats to herself, attempting to re-establish the categories that were imperiled by the Caves. Though she has been a freethinker, she turns to Jehovah for redress: "God who saves the King will surely support the police," goes her reasoning (p. 211). From the day of the hallucination until the climax of the trial she continually seeks to reconstruct the incident in direct logical terms. The dark savage has attacked her—but who has been the savage, Aziz or herself? Her virtue has been threatened—or has she simply rebelled against her starched prudery? Justice will be exacted upon the guilty one—but who is to cast the first stone in matters of sex? The psychological complexity of Adela's situation lends a kind of realistic support to Professor Godbole's doctrinal view: "All perform a good action, when one is performed, and when an evil action is performed, all perform it." (p. 177)

Forster would not assert this as a fixed principle, but we have often enough observed him recoiling from its opposite, the black-and-white attribution of guilt and innocence to separate parties. Before Adela can be freed from the echo of the Cave she must retreat a little from her simplistic Western notion of cause and effect. She is finally able to retract her charge because she has achieved a "double relation" to the controversial event: "Now she was of it and not of it at the same time. . . ." (p. 227) In other words, she has begun to feel the limitations of a knowledge that is strictly bounded by her personality, her discrete selfhood. If she is never to know what occurred in the Cave, at least she will remember that there may be an order of truth beyond the field of her rational vision. Like Fielding, whose empiricism has brought him no closer to knowledge than her own resort to prayer, Adela has reached "the end of her spiritual tether . . . Were there worlds beyond which they could never touch, or did all that is possible enter their consciousness? They could not tell. . . . Perhaps life is a mystery, not a muddle; they could not tell. Perhaps the hundred Indias which fuss and squabble so tiresomely are one, and the universe they mirror is one. They had not the apparatus for judging." (p. 263)

A *Passage to India*, then, is a novel in which two levels of truth, the human and the divine, are simultaneously explored, never very successfully. Epistemological conclusions are reached, but they are all negative ones. Christian righteousness, we discover, helps us to misconstrue both God and man; Moslem love can scarcely reach beyond the individual personality; rational skepticism is wilfully arid; and the Hindu ideal of oneness, though it does take notice of the totality of things, abolishes the intellectual sanity that makes life endurable to the Western mind. The inescapable point of this demonstration is that God cannot be realized in any satisfactory way. It is a point that Forster dwelt upon at some length in his earlier novels, but always with a note of smugness; there was always the facile warning that we should restrict our interest to the world that we know. In A *Passage to India*, however, Forster's characters are given no choice; if they are to understand themselves and one another they must grapple with metaphysics. They do their best, but it is very little—not because they are exceptionally weak, but simply because they are human. Forster implies that we ourselves, his readers, are equally blocked off from meaning. We cannot fall back on reason and the visible world, for we see how these are falsely colored by personality. Even if we could, we ought not seek Mrs. Moore's "dignified and simple" identification with the universe, for this is nihilism in disguise. Nor can we assert with humanistic piety that our whole duty is to love one another; this, too, proves more difficult than we might have gathered from Forster's previous books. What finally confronts us is an irreparable breach between man's powers and his needs.

It is perhaps significant that Forster's career as a novelist comes to an apparent end at this moment of development, for the characters of a novel, as he has said elsewhere, "suggest a more comprehensible and thus a more manageable human race; they give us the illusion of perspicacity and power." (*Aspects of the Novel*, p. 99) *A Passage to India*, though it tells us more about its characters than they themselves know, tries to refute the very thought that our race is comprehensible and manageable; it casts doubt upon the claim of anyone, even of the artist, to supply the full context of human action. In writing one novel which pays full deference to the unknown and the unknowable, Forster thus seems to announce the end of the traditional novel as he found it; between pathetic futility and absolute mystery no middle ground remains for significant action.

Eleven

THE IMPORTANCE OF REASON

The most important element in Forster's sensibility—the one that plainly distinguishes him from most other liberals and humanists—is his overriding eclecticism. The most active force in his novels is his belief that the human mind is an undignified organ: that man cannot be both "impressive and truthful"[1] at the same time. The principle applies to Forster's own efforts at "impressiveness" as well as to those of his characters. In his novels, where his ideals are not simply announced but acted upon and tested for practicability, no faith stands up very well—not even the humanistic faith proclaimed in *Abinger Harvest* and *Two Cheers for Democracy*. Rickie Elliot, who of all his characters is the closest to Forster, is spiritually ruined by his desperate search for value, and Cyril Fielding, the ideal liberal, comes to wonder whether his tolerance and brotherhood have brought him toward any goal. The most successful of Forster's humanists, Margaret Schlegel, succeeds precisely to the degree that she refrains from demanding that her ideals be mirrored in the world. She adopts Forster's own posture of standing ready to alter his interpretation of reality at a moment's notice.

Each of Forster's novels, we might say, gets its total structure of plot from this eclecticism. In each case we are presented with idealistic characters whose original dreams are more impressive than truthful—Philip Herriton's idea of Renaissance glory, Rickie's ethereal classicism, Margaret's vision of cooperation between business and culture, Aziz and Fielding's notion of interracial understanding. In most cases something of the ideal is salvaged, but the original impressiveness is always lost.

[1] See especially *Aspects of the Novel*, p. 212.

Forster's most sensitive and open-minded characters, if they survive their ordeals at all, emerge with a chastened humanism, an awareness of imperfection and danger; and the business of his novels is just this hacking away of intellectual pretensions. Even Lucy Honeychurch and Stephen Wonham, whose fortunes improve as their characters develop, leave behind them two "impressive" illusions of superiority to the general fate of mankind. Lucy is taught that she cannot ignore either love or death; in marrying into the Emerson family she accepts not only sexual passion but a frank view of man's evanescence, unveiled by religious or social consolations. And Stephen, who has considered himself independent of the past and future, acquires a rudimentary sense of tradition and a feeling of paternal obligation. He too, in other words, emerges with a revision of his first, oversimplified view of reality.

The closer we get to the texture of Forster's novels, the more pervasively we see the eclectic principle in operation. His multiple ironies of plot and his famous (or infamous) casual revelations of his characters' sudden deaths contribute to a deliberate atmosphere of instability and recoil from specious certainties. The everpresent moral of his novels is that nothing is to be taken for granted, that the world must always be interpreted afresh. If, in reading the opening pages of *Where Angels Fear to Tread*, we suspect that Forster is scornful of the Herritons' purely social criteria for marital happiness, we suppose that Lilia will refute them by being happy with Gino; but no—erotic preconceptions turn out to be as risky as social ones. If we mistrust the "outer" worlds of the Pembrokes and the Wilcoxes, we find that the inner worlds of Rickie and Helen have their limitations, too. Margaret's "continuous excursions into either realm" are thrust upon us by Forster himself until, ideally, we have adopted his own double perspective on the world.

This process of complication and revision does not necessarily leave us in Mrs. Moore's spiritual muddledom. As Hyatt Waggoner has argued, the surprises and coincidences in Forster's plots serve to remind us of powers beyond the grasp of Forster's Lilliputian characters.[2] The higher order is not necessarily a friendly one; "those agitating apparitions" that inject disquiet into the "Game of Life" are of consolation only to those who are offended by anthropomorphic religion. Yet this is precisely Forster's situation. "For some of us who are non-Christian," we recall, "there still remains the comfort of the nonhuman, the relief, when we look up at the stars, of realising that they are uninhabitable." This is not precisely nihilism, but a reassurance that man's ability to degrade the universe by humanizing it is limited. If we stumble into farcicality by regarding our lives in a panoramic context of heaven and hell, so, conversely, we may increase our dignity by refusing to do so, by paying homage to the truly unknowable.

This is why a book like *Howards End*, which ostensibly deals with human relationships and the social order, is saturated with allusions to infinity and eternity. In order to become heroic, Margaret must not simply master the crisis of her private life. She must obtain a spiritual flexibility that will exclude neither the human realm of meaning nor the overarching, mysterious one. And this is true of the four other novels as well. When we get to *A Passage to India* the transcendent order or chaos is more sharply hostile to human values than before, but the moral formula is the same; Fielding and Adela depart from the ranks of the misguided blunderers only when they have acknowledged that they lack "the apparatus for judging" whether life is a mystery or a muddle. Intellectual maturity among Forster's characters is always prefaced by metaphysical humility.

Forster's eclecticism, then, is something more than an automatic vibration, a habit of timidity; it is his method of coping with a fundamental problem of knowledge. To see his mental logic we must bear in mind a distinction between his sense of

[2] Hyatt Howe Waggoner, "Exercises in Perspective: Notes on the Uses of Coincidence in the Novels of E. M. Forster," *Chimera*, III, No. 4 (Summer 1945), 3-14.

reality and his sense of value; between the uninhabitable stars and the yearning for individual human meaning. It is in the nature of Forster's humanism that these two senses should work against each other. In *The Longest Journey*, where they are most violently in conflict, Forster's moral point is that we should persist in our humanism despite our sense of futility; the enormous difference between man's ideal hopes and his actual circumstances is the energizing force of the novel. And if *A Passage to India* offers a kind of grim stasis instead of energy, it is because Forster has allowed one of his senses almost to throttle the other. His eclecticism is finally tipped over on the side of irony and disillusion—evidence enough, I should think, that he is responsive to the world's complexity and is not simply performing intellectual gymnastics.

Forster's present reputation, so far as one can judge, has been affected by ideological considerations as much as by artistic ones. He is so much the committed liberal, in spite of his eclecticism, that critics have tended to praise or blame him according to their approval or disapproval of liberalism. Though this is unfortunate, the questions raised are by no means irrelevant. Posterity may conceivably be capable of "purely aesthetic" judgments, but aesthetic value itself, at least in the novel, is dependent on a moral and perceptual soundness in the writer. We have to ask, therefore, whether Forster's liberalism is of the sort that makes for a weak grasp of reality.

The argument against liberalism takes many forms—at least as many forms as there are contradictory accounts of what liberalism is—but we may divide them roughly into political and moral criticisms. The political ones need not detain us, since they are irrelevant to Forster personally. When Harold Laski, for example, says that liberal theory merely cloaks the profit motive with respectability and smooths the way to totalitarianism, he is thinking of Henry Wilcox's liberalism, not Forster's.[3] Liberalism in

[3] See Harold J. Laski, *The Rise of Liberalism; The Philosophy of a Business Civilization* (New York and London, 1936), *passim*. For his

Forster is not an adjunct of capitalism but a code of moral value.

The most coherent objections to this code spring from the traditional Christian view of human nature, of which we may take T. S. Eliot as an advocate. Eliot believes that liberalism is a kind of moral paralysis, a system of negation that erases valuable distinctions of class and doctrine. The political chaos of the modern world, in this view, is attributable to the success of such liberal errors as "progress," egalitarianism, and the denial of original sin. Mr. Eliot has explicitly stated the literary consequence of this position: we must disapprove of works that fail to reflect the (apparently obvious) "primacy of the supernatural over the natural life."[4] By this standard, of course, Forster's novels are worthy only of contempt. While they do not embody the liberal materialism hidden in the nineteenth-century idea of progress, they do rest on a foundation of secularism and individualism that Eliot considers pernicious.[5]

Eliot's basic plea, that we concern ourselves with the philosophical or theological framework of a work of literature, is not unreasonable. We have the right to demand of an author that he show us some interpretation of life beyond the mere recording of data. Whether we must therefore subscribe to Mr. Eliot's brand of supernaturalism, however, is another question. In this century it would seem to be essential to literary creativeness that an author *not* accept an a priori interpretation of the meaning of things. I cannot think of a single great modern work, including *The Waste Land*, that has been written in a spirit of orthodoxy. When we bring together Proust, Mann, Gide, Yeats,

alleged failure to see through capitalistic liberalism, Forster is attacked by D. S. Savage, *The Withered Branch; Six Studies in the Modern Novel* (London, 1950), p. 47.

[4] T. S. Eliot, "Religion and Literature," *Selected Essays* (New York, 1950), p. 352.

[5] For samples of the Eliotic approach to Forster, see Montgomery Belgion, "The Diabolism of Mr. E. M. Forster," *The Criterion*, XIV (1934), 54-73, and Peter Ault, "Aspects of E. M. Forster," *The Dublin Review*, CCXIX (1946), 109-134.

Joyce, and Lawrence we have collected as weird a conglomeration of what R. P. Blackmur calls "irregular metaphysics" as could be found anywhere. Indeed, if Forster is not named to the literary pantheon it may be because his vision of reality is not irregular enough.

Discounting Eliot's partisanship, however, we remain faced with an important challenge in his rejection of liberalism. The matter to be settled is whether a liberal view of human nature is not narrow-minded and latently anarchistic. Is it not dangerous to imply, as Forster's novels do, that virtue can be upheld apart from faith in a heavenly order of reward and punishment? Does Forster overlook the inherent sinfulness of mankind?

In one sense Forster's works invite criticism of this sort. It is true, certainly, that his picture of man is more optimistic than the Christian one, and conspicuously more so than that of Calvinism. If it is wrong to believe that sources of human goodness can be tapped without the aid of Divine Grace, then Forster is wrong. He is not, however, a Godwinian denier of personal evil, nor can he rightly be grouped with Utopian "ethical scientists" like Leslie Stephen. At times, indeed, Forster alludes to human weakness in virtually a Christian sense. Freedom is menaced today, he has written, "because a million years ago Man was born in chains," and if we are to understand our troubles we must peer "deep into the abyss of our own characters." (*Two Cheers*, p. 9) This insistence on personal responsibility is, as we saw in Chapter Two, the essential point in Forster's approach to social and political issues. And the one moral desideratum underlying all others in his novels is the virtue of self-knowledge—the knowledge of one's limitations and biases as well as of one's power. Far from celebrating an emancipation from religious ties, the novels seek to find the connections that really subsist between man's moral nature and the forces of good and evil that he meets in his world. This, I take it, is the philosophic ideal of religion.

Forster is un-Christian, not because he is irreligious, but because Christianity fails to meet his idea of religious truth. Being skeptical of divine interest in human affairs, he doubts the legitimacy of Christianity's incarnation and miracles. Being eclectic, he finds its intolerance of heresy unappealing. As a student of the classics and of history, he deplores its contempt for secular truth. Because he sees a measure of goodness within the natural world, he dissents from Christian otherworldliness and hatred of carnality. And because he finds no historical evidence that Christianity has brought men any closer to peace and mutual understanding than they were in classical times, he does not take the moral influence of its doctrines very seriously. There is no Rousseauistic naïveté behind these judgments. To doubt the efficacy of Christian redemption is not automatically to stake one's faith in impulses from a vernal wood, and to uphold the value of a civilized individualism is not to deny the evil that really does infect the world. Forster does not approach the depth of a Dostoyevsky in penetrating into the darker part of man's soul, but neither does he ignore its existence and its potential terrors.

The severest reservations about Forster's outlook come from a direction that is harder to define than the Christian one; it is moralistic but at the same time it upholds the priority of "real life" over any moral pattern. I am thinking of F. R. Leavis and his followers, the sworn enemies of aestheticism and intellectuality in general and of Bloomsbury in particular. As opposed to G. E. Moore's "complex wholes" of consciousness, these critics believe in sexual vitality, in emancipation from effete leisure-class traditions, and in the importance of moral choices leading to the life of useful action. Thought divorced from action—as found, for example, in Laurence Sterne and the later Henry James—is repugnant to this school.[6] While Leavis himself has had kind

[6] See especially F. R. Leavis, *The Great Tradition* (Garden City, New York, 1954), pp. 11n., 188-210.

words for Forster, mingled with detraction,[7] his followers have considered Forster a dilettante and a dreamer, in contrast to their earnest and passionate hero, D. H. Lawrence.

It is difficult to appreciate the real import of the Leavisite charges against Bloomsbury without an awareness of the social antagonism that generates them. One has the impression in reading the *Scrutiny* critics that the class war is being fought over the prostrate body of literature. When *Hard Times* is declared to be Dickens' masterpiece,[8] for example, one feels that something other than literary value must be involved. For all this, Leavis' assault on the "intellectual aristocracy" has probably been a spur to creativity in England, and as an outsider I am certainly not in a position to condemn it. It may simply be doubted whether Leavis' specific complaints against Bloomsbury are always well-founded. Superciliousness, idleness, worship of aesthetic enjoyment—these, within limits, are genuine Bloomsbury traits, and when carried to extremes they do isolate the artist from the real world that should nourish his art. But the Leavisite school seems to exaggerate the contrast between its own moral energy and Bloomsbury's studied amorality. The Bloomsbury disdain for acquisitiveness was, after all, the consequence of a moral review of the hypocrisies latent in *laissez faire*, self-help, and limited Christian philanthropy. The careers of Leonard Woolf and J. M. Keynes prove that Bloomsbury figures could engage themselves in the world, and Forster's own detachment from politics goes back to a broad ideal of individualism, not to class snobbery.

Whether or not Forster would have been a better man if he had been raised in a working-class atmosphere is, of course, beyond our interest here. The point to be considered is whether his particular kind of detachment has impaired his grasp of reality as a novelist. It seems to me, indeed, that Forster's eclecticism

[7] See, F. R. Leavis, "E. M. Forster," *The Common Pursuit* (London, 1952), pp. 261-277.
[8] See *The Great Tradition*, p. 273.

does not spare him from a certain shallowness that is inherent in his liberalism. His hypersensitivity to the compromising nature of action and his tendency to draw an impassable line between individuals and "society" lead him into sentimentality over the holiness of the individual. It is not so much that Forster really finds the individuals he meets "divine" as that his aversion to every show of corporate power leaves him with nothing to cling to *but* an abstract and artificial notion of individuality.

It is a commonplace of modern psychology that an individual man is a locus of warring influences emanating from his parents, his environment, and his own divided psyche; however much force his "individuality" may show, it gains its shape and direction from the resolution of these various pressures. This means that it is no longer plausible to worship the "unprejudiced individual" in the manner of John Stuart Mill, or even to accept without qualification Mill's theory about the victory of truth in a "free" society. We have discovered that attractively packaged and persistently advertised falsehoods have greater appeal than plainly-wrapped truths; the supposedly rational individual can be seduced from his opinions in various subliminal ways. Forster, however, cannot afford to absorb such knowledge, though he has duly taken note of it. He is determined to see the individual as separate and whole, a miraculous being who might accomplish "the service that is perfect freedom" if only he were left unhampered by society.[9] It does not occur to Forster that this figure is nothing more than a dream of the liberal imagination—one that has inspired good works, but which serves poorly as a model for realistic characters in fiction. Insofar as Forster's social and intellectual background has blinded him to this, the Leavisite critics seem justified in their class-conscious attacks.

The restrictive effect of Forster's liberalism is plainly visible in his early novels. Each of them turns upon a romantic polarity

[9] See *Two Cheers*, p. 10.

between the characters' "true selves" and their social milieu. Society is rendered almost as a conscious force for the obstruction of self-development and the inculcation of lies about duty and propriety. To win Forster's approval the characters must not simply become true to themselves, but must utterly reject the enfeebling bourgeois code of their friends; and though Forster's plots make this rejection seem difficult to the characters, it seems all too easy to the reader. There is no trick to seeing through the Reverend Eager or Harriet Herriton, and the novels in which they appear are uncomfortably close to farce. In *The Longest Journey*, where moral seriousness is essential, the important figure of Herbert Pembroke is virtually a caricature. We are asked to believe that the intelligent and sensitive Rickie is torn between Herbert's world and the individualistic one of Ansell and Stephen, but this is scarcely believable; Forster has blackened "society" so zestfully that Rickie's dilemma seems thin and melodramatic. And we have noted how the tolerant theme of *Howards End*, instead of fundamentally modifying Forster's attitudes, merely creates a strain between his intention and his true feelings. It is simply impossible for him to give society its due.

Forster's reverence for the private life, then, often obstructs his efforts at moral realism. His novels before A *Passage to India* approach the condition of fable; their secondary characters tend to be schematic opposites to one another, and their heroes move among these characters as a knight in *The Faerie Queene* might shuttle between enslavement to vices and allegiance to virtues. In *Where Angels Fear to Tread* and *A Room With a View* we may say that this effect is intentional; these books are governed more by comic justice than by psychological realism. In *The Longest Journey* and *Howards End*, though, Forster is committed to a serious representation of actuality; here, it seems, his romantic liberalism leaves him with types of "the world" that are too close to allegorical pawns. It is not that such characters as Herbert Pembroke and Henry Wilcox fail to resemble real people, but that Forster's antipathy to them is so glaringly evident that we cannot share the other characters' sympathetic interest in them. We see at once that their real function is to become the straw men in an argument against inhibition.[10]

This leads us to the general reflection, explicitly made by Leavis, that Forster's desire to "say things" through his characters frequently causes him to violate plausibility of motivation. Not only does Forster himself preach at us from time to time and subject us to the moralizing of an Anthony Failing or a Mr. Emerson, but the central characters themselves are given didactic roles. The virtually incessant philosophizing of Rickie, Ansell, and Stephen makes for an overbalance of theme at the expense of characterization in *The Longest Journey*; Ansell, for instance, exists simply in order to refute the Pembrokes. In *Howards End* the entire plot seems to be an intellectual contrivance for the illustration of a theme; the Wilcox-Schlegel marriage is allegorically significant but psychologically artificial, and the connection of the Basts to both houses is too appropriate to be considered literal. That Forster's novels are thematically coherent is admirable, of course, but we would prefer that the themes appear to grow out of the characters rather than the reverse. In reading Forster we never have the feeling, so superabundant in Joyce, that the sheer reality of the characters is more striking than any intellectual or moral value they might convey.

The mention of Joyce may prove helpful to us at this point, for Joyce's strength and weakness are conspicuously opposite to Forster's. Both writers express disapproval of the ascetic discrimination between body and soul.[11] In *Ulysses*, however, Joyce's anti-asceticism can be felt in the texture of the language; we see, hear, taste, smell, and touch the interdependence of the physical and the spiritual. We feel ourselves in the pres-

---

[10] Forster apparently agrees: "The goats and sheep are too plain, surely," he told Angus Wilson. See *Encounter*, No. 50 (November 1957), 53.

[11] For this intention of Joyce in *Ulysses*, see Richard Ellmann, *James Joyce* (New York, 1959), p. 450.

ence of a world whose overpowering immediacy seems to thrust interpretive questions into the background. It is impossible, for instance, to pause at any point in *Ulysses* and make an intelligent surmise as to what will happen next. The sentences roll out with the richly arbitrary sequence of our unconscious thoughts; they seem at first to invite not analysis but simply awe. And if, on a more sophisticated reading, we see that the novel conceals myriad puzzles and solutions, the total impression remains one of prolific spontaneity.

Forster, on the contrary, is incapable of surprising us very deeply. In his novels the unpredictability of experience is overtly stated and is frequently embodied in a neatly ironic illustration, but it is rarely felt on the level of language. Forster's sentences, instead of exploding in multiple suggestions of meaning, hit their mark with minute precision. They have, in other words, already been sharpened by a fastidious intelligence, and if the reader is alert he will feel their whole meaning at once. Such a style (its prototype is the style of Jane Austen) lends itself supremely to verbal wit and comic irony, and it can convey a steady moral scrutiny of everything it touches. On the other hand, it will not descend to catch the note of experience, but must constantly be selecting and evaluating, even when the author is striving for realism. If Joyce, in his effort to be ingenious and comprehensive, races toward incoherence, Forster too readily withdraws to lucid commentary. While his characters are singing the praises of freedom, passion, and earthiness, his style remains indoors among the teacups.

The virtues of Forster's novels are thus simply the virtues of his intellect: honesty, incisiveness, sympathy, irony, rigor. In Joyce, on the contrary, the conscious operation of intellect always threatens to smother what is truly valuable, the fusion of lyricism with concrete detail. The greatness of *Ulysses*, one might say, is due not only to its author's genius with words, but to the arrogance and superstition that enabled him to charge every moment of experience with significance; while Forster's works, so immediately familiar and congenial, ultimately become imprisoned in their tastefulness. Joyce in his recklessness, his vulgarity, his ferocious independence stretches the limits of art. Forster puts on no airs, takes few chances, and follows out his limited intentions with professional deftness—and so falls short of Joyce.

To say that a modern novelist is not to be ranked with Joyce, however, is not to say much against him. Comparisons of literary merit between Joyce and Forster have little value, since we go to the two writers with such different expectations. And the same remark applies to Forster's other great "competitor," D. H. Lawrence. Lawrence refuses to offer us well-made novels in the Jamesian mode; as Francis Fergusson maintains, Lawrence "was the kind of romantic poet whose writings are seldom self-consistent creations, but rather signs of his inspiration, which is itself the important thing."[12] However romantic Forster may be in feeling, as a plot-maker he is a classicist. We would be surprised to come across any rapturous "epiphanies" in his work; what we do expect is that every scene will be artfully geared to the total structure of development, and that the full meaning of the novel will become apparent only when the development has been brought to its final point.[13]

It could of course be argued on traditional novelistic grounds that Forster's books are incomparably superior to Lawrence's. If

[12] Francis Fergusson, "D. H. Lawrence's Sensibility," *Critiques and Essays on Modern Fiction 1920-1951*, ed. John W. Aldridge (New York, 1952), p. 328.
[13] See *Aspects of the Novel*, p. 133: "The plot-maker expects us to remember, we expect him to leave no loose ends. Every action or word ought to count; it ought to be economical and spare; even when complicated it should be organic and free from dead matter. It may be difficult or easy, it may and should contain mysteries, but it ought not to mislead. And over it, as it unfolds, will hover the memory of the reader . . . and will constantly rearrange and reconsider, seeing new clues, new chains of cause and effect, and the final sense (if the plot has been a fine one) will not be of clues or chains, but of something aesthetically compact, something which might have been shown by the novelist straight away, only if he had shown it straight away it would never have become beautiful."

some of Forster's characters are thin, many of Lawrence's are much thinner—empty receptacles, like Kate Leslie in *The Plumed Serpent*, to be poured full of Lawrentian doctrine. If Forster moralizes now and then, Lawrence subjects us to repetitious barrages of polemics. Where Forster gradually unfolds his theme, Lawrence multiplies illustrations of a few overtly stated ideas. Yet the point is that Lawrence can compel us, partly by his evocative language and partly by the contagiousness of his terrible sincerity, to ignore his technical faults and accept him on his own Dionysian terms.[14] No such force of sheer personality weighs on us in Forster's writing.

It may be, of course, that Forster's novels will be prized because they do *not* submit to the irrationalism that is now in vogue. This is not for us to decide. In literary judgments, however, good sense generally counts for less than imaginative vigor; the novels to which we return are those that are governed by a powerful and original vision of the world. Perhaps because they are insufficiently free from the naïve optimism that accompanied his liberal heritage, Forster's novels before *A Passage to India* do not seem to measure up to this standard. In *Where Angels Fear to Tread* and *A Room With a View*, Forster has complete mastery of a comic genre, but the genre owes more to Jane Austen than to Forster's *Weltanschauung*. In *The Longest Journey* he does strike out on his own, but not boldly enough; the result is ponderous awkwardness instead of freshness. *Howards End*, though it successfully develops the new themes broached in *The Longest Journey*, suffers from an imperfect reconciliation between Forster's "message" and his sense of reality. Only through tyranny of plot, or perhaps tyranny of symbol, does Forster manage to prop his characters into a hopeful posture at the end; the humanistic slogans sound increasingly hollow as the novel's metaphysical backdrop becomes broader. It

[14] For the correlation between Lawrence's and Nietzsche's Dionysianism, see Graham Hough, *The Dark Sun; A Study of D. H. Lawrence* (London, 1956), p. 257.

is only in A *Passage to India* that Forster succeeds in being consistently faithful to his vision of man's impermanence. This book escapes the limitations of its predecessors because it has those limitations for its subject, and makes of them a solid masterpiece of pessimism.

A *Passage to India* thus strikes me as Forster's sole claim upon posterity. And yet the claim seems to be a substantial one. Since we have already studied this novel in detail, let us simply review its position in Forster's career. The progress of his art, we might say, is a movement from commentary about behavior (moral questions) to statements about reality (existential questions). The two Italian novels, with their rather simple ethical dilemmas and their formal infliction of comic justice upon the unworthy characters, are almost exclusively moral; the metaphysical views of Mr. Emerson, for example, are not tested out but are simply intruded into the narrower issue of Lucy's emancipation from "society." Already in *The Longest Journey*, however, we find that the *meaning* of Rickie Elliot's existence nearly overshadows the moral question of what he should do with his life. Indeed, Rickie's moral choices gain their significance only from an elaborated background of theories about the size, uniformity, and ethical character of the universe; and the clash of these theories, while parallel to the crisis of the plot, begins to assume an independent interest. In *Howards End* this metaphysical preoccupation is continued: Margaret Schlegel cannot control her life until she has widened her sense of truth. But it is precisely to the degree that Forster is seriously pursuing the question of existence that his novel seems forced and brittle; for, as we have seen, his instinctive sense of reality is hostile to the chins-up resolution of his plot. When Forster proclaims hopefully at the end, "Let Squalor be turned into Tragedy" (*Howards End*, p. 330), he is trying to rescue the novel from its own metaphysics—from the conclusion that the human order of meaning is of very small consequence to the universe at large.

Hence the necessity, fulfilled in A *Passage to India*, of a novel that passes beyond humanistic morality to a basically metaphysical critique of man's fate. Forster's last novel, unlike the others, refuses to suggest that we can be saved or damned through our behavior; its main point is that God's will, if it exists at all, cannot be known in human terms. I believe that A *Passage to India* is a great book, not because it takes this line of argument—a bad novel, after all, could have been written in the same spirit—but because in drawing upon Forster's profoundest feelings and building itself around them with bold consistency, it achieves aesthetic freedom. Here at last Forster accepts with his whole imagination the destructive ironies of his humanism, rather than stifling them with ambiguous claims about "hope even on this side of the grave." (*Howards End*, p. 103) The result is a novel whose resources of plot and symbolism work in harmony toward a single end, and whose subdued prose reverberates, like the voice of Mrs. Moore, to swell the night's uneasiness. Forster's theme is now sufficiently grand, and his relationship to it sufficiently controlled, for his novel to stand unsupported by moralizing rhetoric. Ironic understatement, which has always been his most effective manner, is here set free to bring all human endeavor into a single focus of description and evaluation.

I should insist, finally, that this triumph of self-criticism does not constitute a betrayal of the liberal humanism that pervades the earlier novels. The essence of that humanism, as it is expressed in the "coinage" chapter of *The Longest Journey*, is a pessimistic awareness of the disparity between human meaning and supernatural truth: a sense not only of the futility of otherworldliness, but of the instability of earthly value. The humanist is portrayed from the first as the owner of a paralyzing knowledge of man's limitations, a seeker after truth who knows that he is ill-equipped to make sense of the world. A *Passage to India* makes us feel the pathos of this condition more vividly than its predecessors, for it refuses to glamorize the relatively slight reassurance that is left to the humanist when he has turned his back on heaven. The original picture, however, is not essentially changed. Forster's last novel merely emphasizes more vividly the impossibility—except perhaps in art—of victory over fortune and time. Humanistic tolerance and sympathy remain the cardinal Forsterian virtues, but they lead to no splendid reward and must simply be exercised in the absence of any better way of getting along.

If A *Passage to India* is, as I believe, incomparably superior to the rest of Forster's fiction, it is nevertheless not a tour de force. It is, rather, the culminating expression of Forster's refinement of liberalism. Like *The Magic Mountain*, also published in 1924, it expresses the self-scrutiny of a mind that is anchored in liberalism and yet aware of weaknesses in the liberal tradition. Like Mann, Forster rests his masterpiece on a foundation of intellectual integrity; his nearly suicidal eclecticism becomes a weapon for aesthetic victory over the partiality and error it reveals. The victory belongs to reason, but to reason defining the limits of reason. We could see in such novels, if we wished, the formal surrender of liberalism to the self-doubts that have always tormented it; but we may see them equally as announcing the severance of liberal ideals from the narrow dogmas of progress and profit. Forster's career as a novelist, in any case, finally brings him away from the fashionable slogans of sexual equality, self-expression, and even social responsibility, and places him briefly in the company of those great writers who have looked steadily, with humor and compassion, at the permanent ironies of the human condition.

INDEX

Index

Allen, Glen O., 155, 157n.
Annan, Noël, 7 and n., 12n., 44n.
Apollo and Apollonianism, 124-125, 127-130, 133, 140-141
"Apostles, The," 40-41
Arnold, Matthew, 8n., 16, 27, 31, 34n., 35 and n., 125
Auden, W. H., 16
Ault, Peter, 168n.
Austen, Jane, 96-97, 99, 175, 177

Bagehot, Walter, 27
Beal, Anthony, 109n.
Beethoven, Ludwig van, 89, 120
Belgion, Montgomery, 168n.
Bell, Clive, 8n., 44, 47
Bell, Vanessa, 10n., 44
Bentham, Jeremy, 25-28, 47n., 118
Berenson, Bernard, 8n.
Berkeley, Bishop George, 61
Bible, 53, 78 and n., 100
Blackmur, R. P., 169
Bloomsbury Group, The, 8n., 10, 17-18, 25, 28, 42n., 43-49, 170-171
Botticelli, Sandro, 89-90
Brookfield, Frances M., 41n.
Brown, Alan W., 41n.
Brown, E. K., 3, 54n.
Brown, Norman O., 157, 158n.
Browning, Robert, 71, 125
Buddhism, 43
Bunyan, John, 137
Bush, Douglas, 125n., 131n.
Butler, Samuel, 27, 95-96, 99, 140
Byron, George Gordon, Lord, 56n.

Calvinism, 169
Cambridge University, 3, 10, 11, 19, 29, 31, 39-50, 53, 55, 56, 57, 61, 62, 127-128, 131, 134, 146
Carlyle, Thomas, 11, 82, 143
Carpenter, Edward, 21
Chamberlain, Joseph, 29
Chaucer, Geoffrey, 104
Chesterton, G. K., 32-34, 107

Clapham Sect, 8-13, 18, 24, 40, 47
Clerk-Maxwell, James, 41
Clifford, W. K., 11n.
Communism, 20, 23n., 35
Conrad, Joseph, 147
Cornford, F. M., 8n.

Dante Alighieri, 79
Darwin, Charles, 8n., 12
Demeter, 135-137, 138, 140
Dicey, A. V., 12
Dickens, Charles, 171
Dickinson, G. L., 29-30, 39, 41-43, 47-49, 50, 96, 131
Dionysus and Dionysianism, 124-132, 141, 177 and n.
Discussion Society, The, 43 and n.
Disraeli, Benjamin, 28
Dostoyevsky, Fyodor, 170

Eliot, T. S., 4, 128, 149, 168-169
Ellmann, Richard, 174n.
Emerson, R. W., 62
Ensor, R. C. K., 28n.
Erasmus, 13

Fabianism, 21, 48
Fascism, 20-23
Fawcett, Henry, 11, 27
Fergusson, Francis, 176
Fielding, Henry, 97
Forster, Alice Whichelo, 8, 152
Forster, Rev. Charles, 7-8
Forster, Edward, 8
FORSTER, E. M.
    admiration for the Greeks, 17, 42-43, 131; ancestry and family tradition, 7-10, 23-24, 38, 44, 110; development of career, 3-6, 20, 50, 67-71, 72-73, 91, 101-104, 105, 122-124, 163, 167, 173, 178-180; eclecticism, 13-14, 39, 48, 73-74, 92-96, 127, 164-167, 171-172, 180; faith in personal relations, 5, 37-38, 41-42, 47-49, 106, 109-